AF270594

THE WATTS FAMILY MURDERS

BY CARLA MOONEY

AMERICAN
CRIME
STORIES

Essential Library

An Imprint of Abdo Publishing | abdobooks.com

ABDOBOOKS.COM

Published by Abdo Publishing, a division of ABDO, PO Box 398166, Minneapolis, Minnesota 55439. Copyright © 2024 by Abdo Consulting Group, Inc. International copyrights reserved in all countries. No part of this book may be reproduced in any form without written permission from the publisher. Essential Library™ is a trademark and logo of Abdo Publishing.

Printed in the United States of America, North Mankato, Minnesota.
102023
012024

Cover Photos: RJ Sangosti/The Denver Post/Getty Images (Watts); Shutterstock Images (tank)
Interior Photos: Lewis Geyer/Digital First Media Group/Boulder Daily Camera/ MediaNews Group/Getty Images, 5, 12, 60; David Zalubowski/AP Images, 7, 40, 63, 73; RJ Sangosti/The Denver Post/Getty Images, 10, 28, 43, 69, 81, 96; Netflix/Everett Collection, 15, 32, 67; RJ Sangosti/The Denver Post/AP Images, 18, 21, 87, 89, 92; iStockphoto, 25, 31; John Greim/LightRocket/Getty Images, 35; Katie Wood/The Denver Post/Getty Images, 44; John M. Chase/iStockphoto, 48; Jacob Boomsma/ Shutterstock Images, 53; RJ Sangosti/MediaNews Group/The Denver Post/Getty Images, 57; Shutterstock Images, 75; Dan Elliott/AP Images, 76; Matt Jonas/Digital First Media Group/Boulder Daily Camera/MediaNews Group/Getty Images, 85; Red Line Editorial, 95

Editor: Laura Stickney
Series Designer: Melissa Martin

Library of Congress Control Number: 2023939440

PUBLISHER'S CATALOGING-IN-PUBLICATION DATA

Names: Mooney, Carla, author.
Title: The Watts family murders / by Carla Mooney
Description: Minneapolis, Minnesota: Abdo Publishing, 2024 | Series: American crime stories | Includes online resources and index.
Identifiers: ISBN 9781098292164 (lib. bdg.) | ISBN 9798384910107 (ebook)
Subjects: LCSH: Crime and criminals--Juvenile literature. | Killing (Murder)--Juvenile literature. | United States--Juvenile literature. | Watts family--Juvenile literature. | Family violence--Juvenile literature. | Colorado--Frederick-- Juvenile literature. | Murderers--Juvenile literature.
Classification: DDC 364.97--dc23

CONTENTS

This book discusses accounts of crime, violence, and death that may be disturbing to some readers.

CHAPTER ONE

MISSING

n the early morning of August 13, 2018, 34-year-old Shanann Watts and her friend Nickole Atkinson returned home from a weekend business trip to Scottsdale, Arizona. The two women were promoters for the lifestyle supplement brand Thrive. Bad weather had delayed their flight home to Colorado, and it was around 2:00 a.m. when Atkinson dropped Shanann off at her home in Frederick, Colorado. Shanann was 15 weeks pregnant.[1] She had not been feeling well throughout the weekend. Atkinson waited until Shanann was inside the house before driving home.

A few hours later, at 7:45 a.m., Atkinson's alarm went off. Still groggy from lack of sleep, she grabbed her cell phone to check for messages. There was nothing from Shanann, which Atkinson found unusual. Shanann, a Thrive team leader, was usually excited to get to work promoting the brand after company business trips. Normally, she would have sent multiple

The Watts family house is located in a suburb about 30 minutes away from Denver. The five-bedroom home is close to a school and playground.

messages to Atkinson by this time. Although she found it strange, Atkinson assumed that Shanann's pregnancy and morning sickness had simply slowed her down that morning. But an hour later, she still had not received any messages from Shanann. In her gut, Atkinson worried something was wrong.

During their trip, Atkinson noticed that Shanann did not have her usual energy and happy demeanor. Instead, Shanann told Atkinson she was worried about her husband, Chris. The couple had been married for six years and were the parents of four-year-old Bella and three-year-old Celeste, with another child on the way. Shanann said Chris no longer wanted their new baby. She suspected he was seeing another woman. Shanann told Atkinson she would talk to Chris about it when she returned home from Scottsdale.

An Uneasy Feeling

All morning, Atkinson tried to reach Shanann. She texted and called, but Shanann did not respond. With each passing minute, Atkinson

Shanann, *right*, was often described as a dreamer and go-getter who had a fiery spirit. Bella, *left*, was known for being shy and cautious, while Celeste, *middle*, was more outgoing.

grew more uneasy. It was not like Shanann to be entirely unresponsive for so long. She was known for being very active on social media, posting on Facebook and texting her Thrive team members multiple times a day.

Atkinson knew Shanann had been looking forward to a doctor's appointment that morning, hoping to hear her baby's heartbeat for the first time. Atkinson called the doctor's office to check on her friend. When the office reported that Shanann had missed the appointment, Atkinson became convinced that something was wrong. At around noon, she jumped into her car with her teenage son, Nicholas, and two-year-old daughter. They drove to the Wattses' home.

Once they arrived at the house, Atkinson rang the doorbell and knocked on the front door. Through the window, she could see Shanann's shoes and luggage in the hall. She shouted Shanann's name several times, but no one answered the door. Atkinson looked in the garage and spotted Shanann's car, which had her daughters' car seats inside.

Unconcerned

Finally, Atkinson called Shanann's husband, Chris. He was an oil field operator for the Anadarko Petroleum company. Chris did not seem concerned that Atkinson could not reach Shanann. He told Atkinson that Shanann had taken their daughters to a playdate at a friend's house, but he did not know the friend's name.

ANADARKO PETROLEUM

Anadarko Petroleum Corporation was a petroleum and natural gas company with operations in the United States, Algeria, Ghana, Colombia, New Zealand, Kenya, and Brazil. It was one of the largest oil and gas drillers in Colorado, operating hundreds of wells in the Denver-Julesburg Basin. This is a rich drilling area that covers Weld County, Colorado, and parts of Wyoming and Nebraska. In 2019, Occidental Petroleum Corporation bought Anadarko Petroleum.

Then Chris told Atkinson that he and Shanann were separating and putting their house up for sale. "Your personal stuff is none of my business," said Atkinson. "That's not my concern right now. But where is your wife?"[3] Chris insisted he did not know. Then he said he was busy at work and hung up the phone. Atkinson found the entire exchange puzzling. Although Shanann and Chris were having issues, Shanann had told Atkinson that she fully expected to work through their problems. "She didn't talk about leaving him or separating. She very much loved her family and wanted to be a family," said Atkinson. "I didn't find out that they were going to separate or anything like that until I called Chris that morning."[4]

While Chris appeared unconcerned about his wife's whereabouts, others were also worried about Shanann. Her mother, Sandra Rzucek, had been unable to reach Shanann all morning. Several friends had also been trying to contact her. One friend, Cassandra Rosenberg, said she was worried when she could not reach Shanann that morning. "Every morning, all of us would hear something from her. She would text and say hello. She was always very open on social media about her life. So not hearing anything that morning, I was like, 'OK . . . ,'" said Rosenberg. "My first instinct was that something happened, being pregnant. You instantly go medical, and think, 'Oh my gosh, maybe she passed out or something. Maybe that's why she's not answering the phone.'"[5]

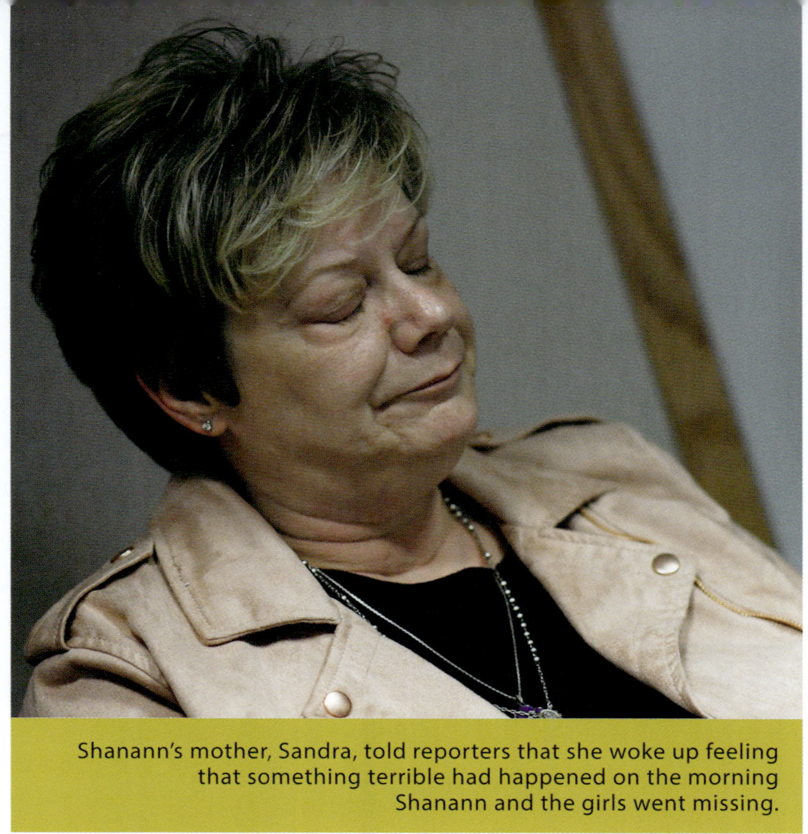

Shanann's mother, Sandra, told reporters that she woke up feeling that something terrible had happened on the morning Shanann and the girls went missing.

Several of Shanann's friends had spoken to or texted Chris. Like Atkinson, they noticed that Chris appeared unconcerned about his pregnant wife. "Anyone in their right mind will start piecing things together and think something had happened," Atkinson said. "But you don't want to go there. You want to believe the best in people."[6]

Calling the Police

Outside the Wattses' home, Atkinson spoke to Rzucek and a few of Shanann's friends on a conference call. She asked what they thought she should do, and they urged her to call the police. At 1:36 p.m., Atkinson called the Frederick Police Department, which transferred her call to the Weld County Dispatch Center. "I'm calling because I'm concerned about a friend of mine," she told the dispatcher. "She's not answering the door, she's not responding to text messages, phone calls. And there's no movement in the house whatsoever."[7]

At 1:50 p.m., Frederick Police Department officer Scott Coonrod arrived at the Wattses' home, where Atkinson was waiting. She explained her concerns about the welfare of Shanann and her daughters. Atkinson said Chris had insisted that his wife and daughters were on a playdate. But Shanann's car, with the children's car seats inside, was still in the garage. Atkinson also pointed out that the shoes her friend wore every day were sitting right inside the front door.

Officer Coonrod told Atkinson to call Chris and ask him for the garage code and permission to enter the home. She called Chris and told him the police were at his house. Watts replied

Neighbors' concerns kick-started the investigation of Shanann, Bella, and Celeste's disappearance. Even neighbors who did not know the Watts family personally became invested in the case.

that he was a few minutes away and asked them not to break down the door.

While they waited for Chris to arrive, Officer

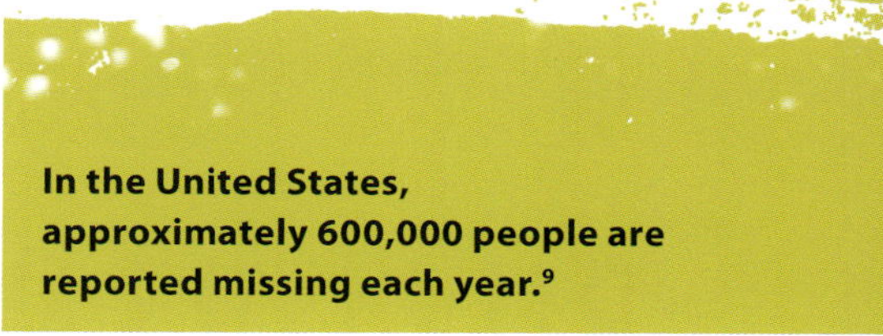

Coonrod circled the house. He knocked on the side of the house and looked in the windows, but no one appeared. Nothing seemed to be out of place. But as they waited for Chris, Atkinson's son, Nicholas, told the officer that he did not trust Chris. "We know he's been lying, because his story's not adding up. He's been telling us a lot of different stories," said Nicholas.[8]

Officer Coonrod made his way back to the front door. He knocked on the door loudly and shouted for Shanann, but there was no response from her or either of her young daughters. The barking of the Wattses' dog, Dieter, was the only sound that could be heard from inside the house.

CHAPTER TWO

BUILDING A LIFE TOGETHER

On January 10, 1984, Shanann Cathryn Rzucek was born to Frank and Sandra Rzucek. Two years later, Shanann's younger brother, Frankie, was born. The family lived in New Jersey, where Shanann and her brother developed a close relationship. As a child, Shanann was insecure and often got bullied at school. Even though Frankie was younger, he took on the role of protector for his sister. He stood up to Shanann's bullies and got into numerous fights for her.

Moving to North Carolina

In 1999, the Rzucek family moved to Aberdeen, North Carolina. Frank Rzucek started a home-improvement business, and Sandra got a job working at a hair salon. Shanann attended Pinecrest High School. At first, she was shy and had trouble

Shanann loved sharing posts about her marriage and family life on social media. In her posts and videos, Shanann often seemed positive, happy, and enthusiastic.

During her senior year of high school, Shanann started dating classmate Leonard King. The couple fell madly in love and married soon after graduation. While some of her friends worried that the couple was too young, Shanann was determined to move forward with her life. "She was adamant about starting her life and having a family. They got married so quickly and she was young and very ambitious," said Colby Cruse, one of Shanann's high school friends.[2]

making friends. But a theater class helped Shanann come out of her shell. She became more comfortable and found a group of friends.

After high school, Shanann married Leonard King, her high school sweetheart. She started college but dropped out and took a job selling cell phones and pagers.

In 2006, Shanann became the manager of a cell phone store in Fayetteville, North Carolina. The store's owner, Hisham Bedwan, had another company called Dirty South. It specialized in car customization. After a few years, Shanann became the bookkeeper for Dirty South and managed its two locations.

Within a few years, Shanann's marriage fell apart. She and her husband divorced in 2007. After her divorce, Shanann moved to Charlotte, North Carolina. By 2009, she was earning a good income. She had a 4,000-square-foot (372 sq m) home built and filled it with top-quality furniture. "She was doing very good [and] she was very business savvy. She was pretty, but she could talk the talk and walk the walk," said Frankie.[1]

However, soon after moving in to her new house, Shanann fell ill. After numerous tests, doctors diagnosed her with lupus. This is an autoimmune disease in which a person's immune system attacks their organs and tissues. Later, doctors also diagnosed Shanann with fibromyalgia, a disorder that causes muscle and bone pain, fatigue, and issues with sleep, memory, and mood. They prescribed medications that made Shanann feel unwell. She could no longer manage Bedwan's stores and quit her job.

While Shanann struggled with her health in July 2010, she received a Facebook message from a man named Chris Watts. He was the cousin of one of Shanann's work colleagues. Chris had messaged her a few months earlier, but Shanann had not responded. This time, however, she did.

LUPUS

Lupus is a complex autoimmune disease that can affect any part of the body. The most common areas affected include the joints, skin, brain, lungs, kidneys, and blood vessels. People with lupus often experience fatigue, joint pain or swelling, skin rashes, and fevers. While anyone can get lupus, nine out of ten people with the disease are women.[3] No one knows what causes lupus, but researchers believe it is a combination of genes and environment. Shanann described getting diagnosed with lupus as the beginning of "one of the darkest times" of her life. She said people "didn't understand that I looked perfectly fine, and . . . felt horribly inside."[4]

A Quiet Young Man

Christopher Lee Watts was born on May 16, 1985, in Fayetteville. His parents, Ronnie and Cindy Watts, say their son was quiet and reserved from a young age. He spent a lot of time with his father and loved sports, cars, and NASCAR races. Ronnie worked as a parts manager for a car dealership and taught Chris about fixing cars.

Chris was shy and withdrawn at school, unlike his outgoing older sister, Jamie. "He didn't go out with friends. I was more of

Before Chris met Shanann, his parents said he was sporty, easygoing, and calm. They believed Chris's personality changed after he became involved with Shanann.

a social butterfly, and he was quiet and interested in mechanics and cars. He was just a focused person," said Jamie. "It was hard to hold a conversation with him unless we were talking about cars," she said.[5]

After his high school graduation in 2003, Chris enrolled in the NASCAR Technical Institute in Mooresville, North Carolina. One day, he hoped to work as part of a NASCAR race team. While in school, Chris worked part time at a car dealership. In 2006, Chris graduated from the NASCAR Institute. He applied for several jobs with NASCAR but was never hired. Instead, Chris worked full time as a service technician at a local car dealership. The job paid well, but Chris's dream of working for NASCAR was crushed.

In 2010, Chris's cousin Nicole Canady suggested that he reach out to her work friend, Shanann Rzucek, who had just ended a bad marriage. Chris decided to take a chance and messaged Shanann on Facebook. At first, he did not get a reply. Months later, in July 2010, Chris sent a second Facebook message to Shanann. This time, she replied.

Early Connection

That summer, Shanann and Chris went on a few dates. Then, in late August 2010, Shanann had a lupus flare-up after a day at the beach. Chris took care of her as they drove back to Charlotte. This convinced Shanann that she had found the man of her dreams. "I met Chris because of those health challenges. Because I got so sick, I let him in. . . . He's the best thing that has ever happened to me," Shanann later said in a video posted on Facebook.[6]

The couple's relationship quickly became more serious. As Shanann's health issues continued to cause her pain and discomfort, she became increasingly dependent on Chris. He accompanied her to doctor's appointments and organized her medications. By the fall of 2010, Chris had moved into Shanann's house.

Family Tensions

In late November 2010, Shanann and Chris invited their families to a cookout at their house. However, the two families did not hit it off. Chris's mother and sister wondered how Shanann and Chris could afford such a large house and expensive lifestyle, especially since Shanann was not working a full-time job. They also felt uncomfortable around Shanann's outspoken mother, Sandra. The tensions were evident on both sides. According to Sandra, Chris's mother said she did not think Shanann loved Chris. But Chris's family mostly kept their concerns to themselves. They wanted Chris to be happy, and Shanann seemed to make him happy.

In February 2011, Shanann's friends Jeanna and Charlie Dietz moved from North Carolina to Broomfield, Colorado.

Cindy Watts believed Shanann isolated Chris from his family. She later described her son's relationship with Shanann as difficult and abusive.

After the Dietzes moved, Shanann stayed in touch with Jeanna. Jeanna was a trained nurse who knew about Shanann's lupus. She told Shanann that the mountain air in Colorado would benefit her health. She urged Shanann to think about moving to the state.

Engaged

In August 2011, Chris proposed to Shanann on the beach, and she said yes. The Rzuceks were excited to welcome Chris into their family. The couple seemed to be in love and made a great team. Over Thanksgiving, Shanann and Chris flew to Colorado and stayed with the Dietz family for a week. It was the first time Chris had met the Dietzes, and he made a good impression on them. "He was very doting. Attentive, kind but shy and introverted. He loved my kids," said Jeanna.[7]

During their visit, Shanann and Chris decided to move to Colorado for Shanann's health. They planned for Chris to move first and find a job while Shanann stayed behind in North Carolina to sell her house. They would stay with the Dietzes until they found a place to live in Colorado. Chris's family was unhappy with this plan. They did not want Chris to move so far away.

Moving to Colorado

In April 2012, Chris moved to Colorado and quickly found a job at a car dealership. While he waited for Shanann to join him, Chris worked hard and saved money for their life together. Although they were physically apart, the couple stayed in constant contact.

Shanann sold the North Carolina house in August 2012 and joined Chris in Colorado. She found a sales job at the car dealership where Chris worked. With her friendly personality, Shanann quickly became the top salesperson at the dealership. Coworkers noticed that Shanann was often bossy to Chris. But Chris appeared happy with the arrangement, since it suited his easygoing nature. In October 2012, Chris and Shanann purchased a new home that was being built in Frederick, Colorado. The large 4,177-square-foot (388 sq m) home was on a quiet street in a new neighborhood.[9] Shanann and Chris stayed with the Dietzes until construction on the home was finished.

Happy Newlyweds

On November 3, 2012, Chris and Shanann married in a ceremony at a Charlotte hotel. Shanann had made it clear that Chris's family was not welcome at the wedding, and his grandmother was the only person from his family to attend. After the wedding, the couple traveled to Myrtle Beach, South Carolina, for a honeymoon.

After their honeymoon, Shanann and Chris returned to Colorado. The newlyweds appeared full of hope and happiness as they started their married life. That winter, Shanann and Chris began trying to have a baby. Doctors warned Shanann that her lupus might prevent her from having a child. But after several months of trying, Shanann became pregnant.

CHAPTER THREE

THE PERFECT FAMILY

n April 2013, Shanann and Chris moved in to their brand-new house in Frederick. The couple was excited to raise a family. In July, Shanann announced her pregnancy on Instagram with the caption "Bella Marie Watts coming this Christmas 2013. So excited." Soon after, Chris called his parents and told them Shanann was pregnant. He had not spoken with them in more than two years.[1] Now he acted as if nothing had happened.

New Parents

Shanann diligently recorded her pregnancy on social media. She posted photos of her growing belly and all the dresses and toys she bought for her unborn daughter. She purchased a top-of-the-line crib with the name "Bella" engraved on it.

The family-friendly town of Frederick is located on the Front Range of the Rocky Mountains. It is known for its many oil and gas wells, some of which are close to residential areas.

She filled the baby's closet with dozens of outfits. She lined shelves with children's books and videos.

Shanann had expensive tastes and charged all her purchases on credit cards. The couple did not seem concerned about the growing debt they were accumulating. "Shanann was living way above her means. She wanted the best of everything," said Chris's father, Ronnie.[2]

On December 17, 2013, Bella Marie Watts was born. Chris was in the delivery room to see his daughter's arrival. A few hours later, Shanann posted a picture of Chris and the baby on social media. She praised the love Chris had for their new daughter.

Bella Watts wanted to be Elsa from the Disney movie *Frozen* when she grew up.

In early January, Cindy and Ronnie flew to Denver to meet their granddaughter. It was the first time they had seen Chris in person since his engagement to Shanann. After their first visit, Ronnie and Cindy would fly to Colorado twice a year. During those visits, Cindy noticed that her son seemed anxious and would drop everything whenever Shanann needed something.

As Chris and Shanann settled into life as new parents, Chris appeared to love being a father. He changed the baby's diapers, fed her with a bottle, and read to her every night before bed. He acted like the perfect father.

Before Christmas 2014, Shanann and Chris signed a car lease for a new Ford Explorer SUV. Between the mortgage, car lease, and other expenses, the couple spent thousands of dollars monthly. They were falling deeper and deeper into debt.

In January 2015, Shanann announced on Instagram that she was pregnant again. A few weeks later, she revealed that the new baby was a girl, whom they planned to name Celeste. Shanann's parents temporarily moved in to the couple's basement in Colorado to help their daughter with her toddler and pregnancy.

Financial Troubles

In June 2015, Shanann and Chris's spending finally caught up with them. They owed $3,000 monthly mortgage payments and $600 car payments. They also had $70,000 in debt, mainly from student loans, credit cards, and medical bills.[3] Chris had

In 2018, Anadarko Petroleum was one of Colorado's biggest oil and gas companies. Chris worked at the company's oil well sites and in a company office building.

taken a higher-paying job as an oil field operator for Anadarko
Petroleum in early 2015. But his salary was still not enough
to pay off all the family's debts. At the time, Chris's job paid
an annual salary of $61,500, while Shanann made $18 per
hour working at the children's hospital call center.[5] To get out
from under the mountain of debt, Shanann and Chris filed
for bankruptcy.

A judge needed to approve the couple's bankruptcy filing.
In August 2015, a federal judge agreed to discharge most of the
couple's debt under the condition that they both complete an
online credit course to learn more about managing finances.
Chris and Shanann took the class and passed. Two months later,
the court discharged their debt.

While Shanann did not tell most people that she and Chris
had filed for bankruptcy, she was honest about it with her
mother and her friend Lauren Arnold. Shanann did not seem
overly concerned about the situation. She said the decision to
file for bankruptcy would be better for their family in the long
term. However, Shanann admitted that the financial problems
had put stress on her marriage and that she and Chris argued
over finances sometimes.

Chris had been surprised by the bankruptcy. Because
Shanann handled the finances, he had not realized the extent
of their financial troubles. Chris admitted that finances added
stress to their marriage, but he did not talk to anyone about it.

He never mentioned bankruptcy or financial problems to his parents.

On July 17, 2015, Shanann gave birth to Celeste Cathryn "CeCe" Watts. Once again, Chris was in the delivery room when his daughter was born. Right away, Celeste was a sickly baby. She was diagnosed with an allergic disorder and would need to be on steroids to help her breathe for her first year.

Promoting Thrive

In January 2016, Shanann signed up as an independent contractor for Le-Vel, a health and wellness company. She worked in direct sales as a promoter for Thrive, one of the company's lifestyle supplements. This decision would change her life. At the time, Shanann worked full time on the night shift at the hospital and then went home to care for her daughters during the day. She was exhausted. Thrive supplements

MULTILEVEL MARKETING

Le-Vel is a health and wellness company that uses a multilevel marketing strategy to sell its products. In multilevel marketing, individual sales representatives sell a product directly to customers, often without a physical store. Individual sales representatives are not paid a salary but instead earn a commission on sales. The sales representatives, or promoters, also recruit new promoters to work on their "team." When a lower-level promoter makes a sale, people with higher job positions earn a portion of the commission.

promised to give users more energy, better mental focus, and improved physical health. Shanann bought some of the supplements and persuaded Chris to take them with her.

Almost immediately, Shanann felt energized after taking Thrive. She began recruiting friends and family to start taking the supplements. Soon she persuaded her parents to try Thrive and had recruited several new customers. On Facebook, Shanann began posting about her personal experience with Thrive. She believed the supplements had relieved her pain,

Shanann and Chris filed for bankruptcy with the United States Bankruptcy Court in Denver. Most of the couple's debts were from student loans or shopping purchases.

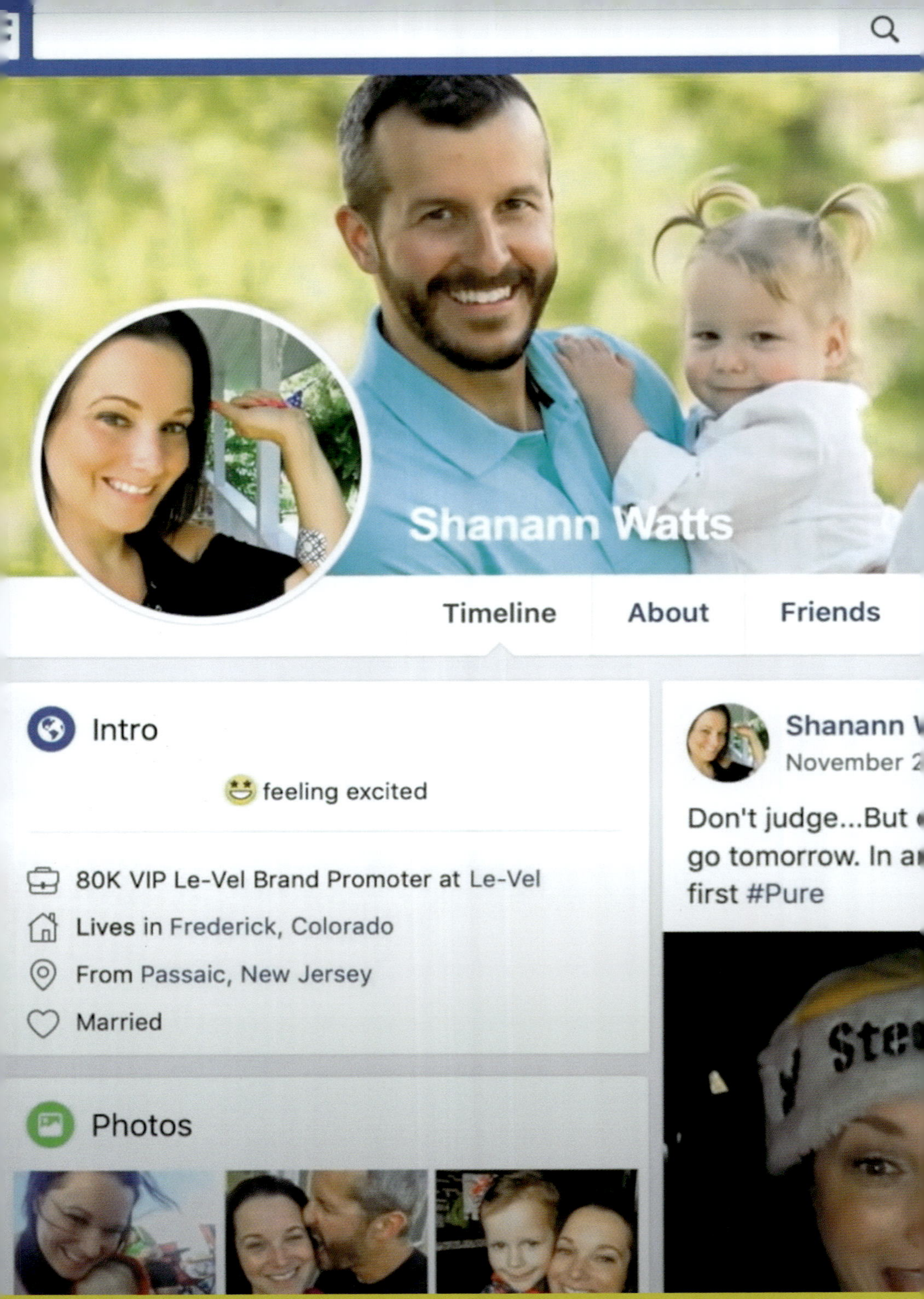

Shanann Watts
Timeline
About
Friends
Intro
feeling excited
80K VIP Le-Vel Brand Promoter at Le-Vel
Lives in Frederick, Colorado
From Passaic, New Jersey
Married
Photos
Shanann
November
Don't judge...But
go tomorrow. In a
first #Pure

Shanann regularly posted on Facebook and other social media platforms, sharing photos of her family and posts about Thrive. She posted several videos of Chris playing with the girls. Investigators would later search Shanann's social media posts for clues about the case.

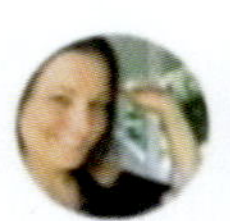

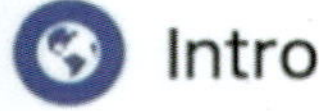

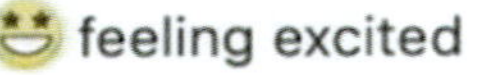

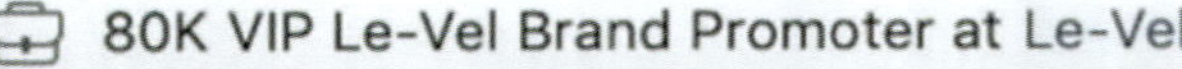

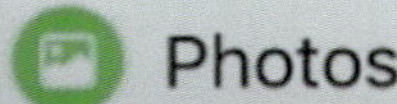

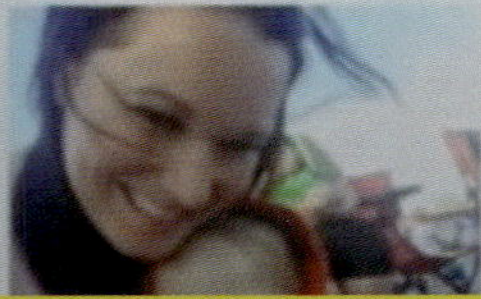

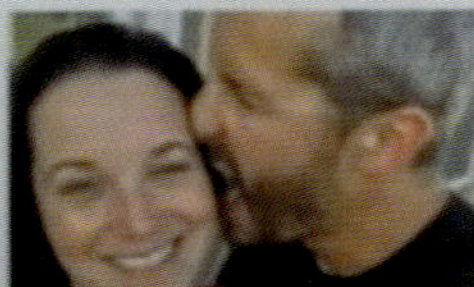

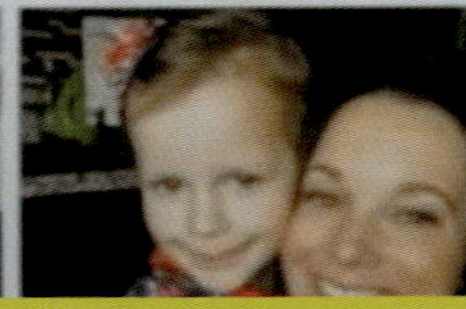

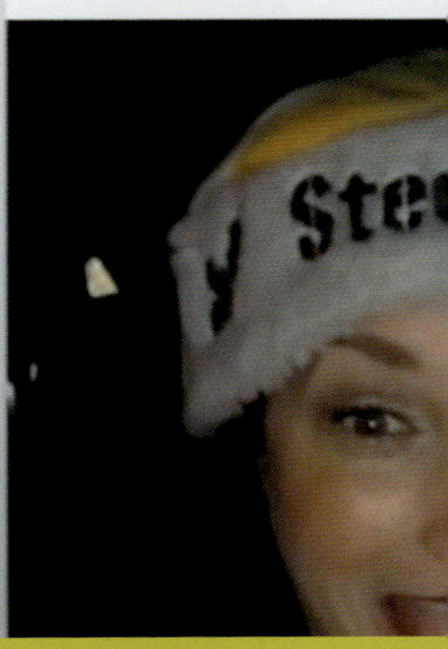

and she said she was able to stop taking her lupus medication.

Within four weeks of promoting Thrive, Shanann had earned more than $1,000 in commissions and a free iPod.[6] Her natural talent for sales paid off, and she steadily increased her sales and commissions. Shanann also established herself in the online Thrive community, where she found new friends who embraced her. On social media platforms such as Facebook, she promoted Thrive while sharing detailed accounts of her life with Chris, Bella, and Celeste. By 2017, Shanann's Thrive business was doing so well that she quit her job at the children's hospital to begin promoting Thrive full time.

A PERFECT LIFE

In her social media posts and videos, Shanann painted the picture of a perfect family. She praised her husband in the posts too. "I couldn't have asked God for a better man in my life because he's so supportive. He takes care of me. He's probably the best father I could have asked for, for my children," Shanann said in one of her Facebook Live videos. "And . . . he completes me. I know that's a cliché, but it's the truth. He completes me."[7] Later, Chris admitted that he hated being on display on social media. But he went along with it because it helped Shanann's business.

CHAPTER FOUR

TROUBLE UNDER THE SURFACE

To the outside world, Shanann and Chris appeared to have it all—two beautiful daughters, a lovely home, and good jobs. Most of all, the couple seemed madly in love. But under the surface of the Wattses' marriage, trouble had been simmering for quite some time.

Health Issues

Shanann, Bella, and Celeste all struggled with numerous health issues, which was stressful for the family. The girls were often sick, and it seemed as if there was one health problem after another for the family to manage. At one point, Shanann posted on Facebook about staying up all night with her sick girls. A few days later, she took Celeste to the hospital to treat a blocked tear duct. Soon after, she took Celeste to the dentist to

On multiple occasions, Shanann took Bella and Celeste to the Children's Hospital in Colorado. During Bella's stay at the hospital for pneumonia, Shanann posted videos of her daughter on social media.

NECK SURGERY

In addition to lupus, Shanann had suffered from migraines for years. By 2017, her migraines had become worse. Shanann scheduled neck surgery to fix a degenerative disc that was pressing on her spinal cord and causing the migraines. Surgeons made a one-inch (2.5 cm) cut in her throat area and removed the disc.[2] They inserted a graft to fuse the bones above and below the disc. Then they screwed a plate to the front of her spine until it healed. While Shanann recovered from the surgery, she wore a neck brace. She was left with a visible scar.

fix a tooth. Then Bella had to be hospitalized for a case of pneumonia.

In December 2016, Celeste had a severe allergic reaction after eating two cashew nuts. She vomited and broke out in a rash. Shanann rushed her daughter to the children's hospital, where doctors observed Celeste for nine hours. They diagnosed her with a severe nut allergy that could cause an anaphylactic reaction, which could be life-threatening. The doctors gave Shanann a device that could be used to inject Celeste with medication if she had another reaction.

Chris often had to take time off work to go to his daughters' doctor's appointments and help his wife care for them. He sometimes spoke about his situation with coworkers. "Both of his kids have been pretty sick over the past couple of years. So he would talk a little bit about the stress that that puts on him and his wife," said Chris's Anadarko supervisor, Luke Epple.[1]

More Financial Troubles

Shanann and Chris appeared to enjoy the finer things in life. They took vacations to places such as Mexico. These trips were often paid for by Shanann's work with Thrive. Shanann also drove expensive cars, including a Lexus and an Audi.

The couple enrolled Bella and Celeste in a private preschool that cost $25,000 a year.[3] Shanann liked shopping too, often spending most of her paycheck on shopping sprees. All the doctor's appointments, hospital visits, and medical treatments for Shanann and the girls added to the family's expenses. Even though the Wattses had declared bankruptcy in 2015, they were still living beyond their means. And their debt was growing again.

By March 2018, the Wattses were three months behind on their mortgage payments and received a warning letter from the bank. They also owed their neighborhood association 12 months of association dues. Shanann had Chris withdraw

$10,000 from his retirement savings account at work to pay the outstanding mortgage payments.[4]

Shanann never mentioned her family's financial troubles on social media. But Chris later said that the mounting debt caused him to feel increasing stress. He worked many hours, but they still always seemed short on money. Chris wondered if they should send the girls to a less expensive school or cut back on some purchases. But he felt that he could not talk to Shanann about their money problems.

A Rocky Relationship

Many people noticed cracks in the Wattses' fairy-tale image. Some said that Shanann could be demanding and bossy toward her husband. Nathaniel Trinastich, a neighbor of the Watts family, often heard Chris and Shanann arguing loudly. "I've heard them flat-out screaming at each other at the top of their lungs, and he gets crazy," said Trinastich.[5]

Another neighbor, Melinda Phillips, witnessed a screaming match between Chris and Shanann one morning while leaving for work. The couple was having an intense argument in their driveway. "Their body language was really angry, and they were just fighting back and forth. He was gesturing his hands and they were shaking their heads, and it was definitely an argument," said Phillips. But when the couple noticed Phillips watching them, the argument quickly stopped. "They caught my eye, and suddenly, everything changed. They stopped being so angry, and they started talking a lot more calmly. He even gave her a hug. Mind you, this was in the space of 30 seconds to a minute. From a full-blown fight to hugs in less than a minute, it was incredible," she said.[6]

A New Baby

In the spring of 2018, Shanann told her friends that she and Chris wanted to have a third child, who they hoped would be a boy. Shanann said Chris was an excellent father to Bella and Celeste and would be great with another baby. As he often did, Chris deferred to his wife's wishes.

But even though Chris told Shanann he wanted another baby, he later admitted that he was unsure about having another child. He was beginning to feel trapped in his marriage, and it bothered him when Shanann criticized him in front of their daughters. Bella and Celeste were starting to repeat their mother's critical words. But instead of talking about his feelings, Chris kept his growing anger to himself.

Shanann's brother, Frankie, was protective of his sister and often worried about her and the girls living so far away.

On May 29, 2018, Shanann set up her phone to film a video in her kitchen. She had a surprise for Chris when he got home from work. She was pregnant. To tell Chris the good news, Shanann wore a T-shirt with the words "Oops . . . we did it again."[7] Wearing the shirt, she filmed Chris as he walked into the kitchen. In the video, Chris stopped to read her shirt and then grinned as the news sank in. He walked over to Shanann and gave her a hug.

Shanann was thrilled to be pregnant again. She called her parents and friends to share the good news. While they shared her excitement, some people, such as Shanann's father, were concerned about how another pregnancy would affect Shanann's health.

In June 2018, Bella was recorded in a video singing "My Daddy is a hero" for Father's Day.[9]

Chris shared the pregnancy news with his parents. "We were shocked," said Cindy. "I thought, 'Well, they must really be doing good to have a third child.'"[8]

On June 1, 2018, days after Shanann had revealed her pregnancy, Chris experienced problems with a computer app he used to control sensors in the oil fields. He went to see Nikki Kessinger, Anadarko's health and safety representative, for help. Although he had noticed Kessinger at work before, it was the first time Chris had spoken to her.

CHAPTER FIVE

THE OTHER
WOMAN

In 2017, Nichol "Nikki" Kessinger was assigned to the Anadarko office as a health and safety representative. Each morning, she walked through the office break room and cafeteria to put her lunch in the refrigerator. Some men waiting for their daily assignments in the break room noticed her. One of those men was Chris. According to his coworker, Anthony Brown, Chris would look up from his laptop and stare awkwardly each day as Kessinger strolled past him. The men often commented on what the young woman was wearing or how she looked. But Chris just smiled and said nothing.

Falling for Nikki

Months later, in June 2018, Kessinger and Chris spoke for the first time. She noticed Chris was not wearing a wedding ring.

When Kessinger first met Chris, she thought he was cute and kind. He seemed like a good father who cared about his kids. Kessinger would later speak to reporters about Chris.

Over the next several days, Kessinger and Chris said hello and exchanged small talk if they happened to pass each other in the office. "When he spoke to me, he was very soft-spoken. He appeared to be a good listener," Kessinger said.[1]

By mid-June, Chris and Kessinger talked regularly, and Chris started opening up to Kessinger about his life. He told her he had moved to Colorado from North Carolina and showed her

The Wyndham Hill Master Association ordered Shanann and Chris to appear at the Weld County Courthouse in Greeley, Colorado.

pictures of Shanann, Bella, and Celeste on his phone. He told Kessinger that he and Shanann were separating, and Kessinger believed him.

On June 26, Chris and Shanann opened a letter from their neighborhood association. It ordered them to appear in court for failing to pay nearly $700 in homeowner's dues.[2] The association had filed a lawsuit against the Watts family to recover the unpaid dues, plus attorney's fees and court costs.

Later that afternoon, Chris drove Shanann, the girls, and his father-in-law to the Denver airport to catch a flight to North Carolina. Shanann had planned a six-week trip to North Carolina with the girls so she could spend time with family and friends. It was the first time the girls would visit North Carolina. Because Chris could not take that much time off work, he would stay in Colorado and join his family in North Carolina a few weeks later.

An Affair Begins

When Chris returned home, he called Kessinger and set a date for the next day. Less than 24 hours after driving his family to the airport, Chris met Kessinger at a nature preserve near her house.[3] It was the first time the two were alone outside of work.

Kessinger asked Chris about his marriage and when he had decided to separate from his wife. He told Kessinger that Shanann was bossy and controlling and that she even made fun of him in front of their daughters. He complained that Shanann often ignored him and spent most of her time on her phone or on social media. Several hours later, Chris and Kessinger went to Kessinger's house and slept together for the first time.

Over the next few weeks, Chris and Kessinger spent almost every night together, usually at her house. Chris was captivated by Kessinger and felt that he could open himself up to her. "She showed him respect that he didn't feel like he'd ever been shown before," said Cheryln Cadle, an author who later exchanged letters with Chris about this period.[4]

Later, Kessinger said she had told Chris that they should take their relationship slowly until his divorce was finalized. "He was like in fifth gear the entire time. Maybe it was up to me to hit the brakes . . . but he was so kind to me . . . why was I going to push him away?" Kessinger said.[5]

As he spent more time with Kessinger, Chris became increasingly

On June 22, Chris and Shanann flew to San Diego for a vacation. The trip was a commission reward that Shanann had earned from Thrive. Shanann's father flew to Denver to stay with the girls while the couple was away. In San Diego, Chris and Shanann had dinner with several friends. During the trip, the couple seemed as happy as ever, and Shanann posted romantic pictures of herself and Chris on social media. While in San Diego, Chris also met up with a longtime friend, Mark Jamieson, who was stationed at the naval base. Chris confessed to Mark that he had been talking to a woman at work. But he did not tell Mark he planned to meet with Kessinger when Shanann was out of town.

distant with Shanann. He ignored most of her calls. And during his nightly FaceTime calls with Bella and Celeste, Chris seemed distracted. Shanann knew that something was different with her husband and marriage, but she did not understand what had changed. She repeatedly questioned Chris about it over text, but he denied that anything was wrong.

Family Tensions

Meanwhile, in North Carolina, another fight erupted between Chris's parents and Shanann. While visiting her in-laws, Shanann discovered that Celeste was about to eat some ice cream that Shanann believed contained traces of nuts. This could have potentially triggered a life-threatening allergic reaction. Shanann had been very clear with her in-laws that Celeste could not be around tree nuts. She accused Chris's mother, Cindy, of trying to kill Celeste. But Cindy insisted that the ice cream was just plain, nut-free vanilla. Furious, Shanann refused to listen. She gathered the girls and called her father to come pick them up.

Back at her parents' house, Shanann immediately called Chris to tell him about the incident. He tried calming her down and assured her that he would handle it. Shanann called Chris again the next day, urging him to confront his parents about the ice cream incident. But Chris hated confrontations. And the more Shanann pushed him, the greater the distance between

During their weekend trip, Chris and Kessinger went sand boarding at Great Sand Dunes National Park. Chris reportedly changed his phone home screen picture from a photo of Shanann and the girls to a photo of the sand dunes.

the couple grew. Chris began avoiding his wife's calls. From that point on, Shanann and Chris communicated mainly through text messages.

Hiding the Affair

As Chris became harder to reach, Shanann became more suspicious of him. Chris rarely answered his phone, even when Shanann's mother called him. When Shanann texted Chris, his replies were sporadic. Frustrated, she texted him, saying,

"I realized [during] this trip what's missing in our relationship! It's only one way emotions and feelings. I can't come back like this. I need you to meet me halfway. You don't consider others at all, nor think about feelings."[6]

At the end of July, Chris and Kessinger took a two-day camping trip to Great Sand Dunes National Park. It was their last weekend together before Chris joined Shanann and the girls in North Carolina. He told Shanann that he was going on a weekend hike with a coworker and would not have cell phone service. On the weekend getaway, the couple took selfies kissing in front of the sand dunes and declared their love for each other.

Distant and Distracted

Two days later, Chris flew to North Carolina to join his family. Shanann and the girls met him at the airport. Although he had not seen his family for five weeks, Chris seemed distant and distracted. Throughout the week, he made excuses to avoid having sex with Shanann and frequently sneaked away to call or text Kessinger. Chris had been looking forward to visiting his parents, but after the ice cream incident, Shanann refused to see them or allow the girls to visit them. Chris was upset that Shanann was causing more problems with his family.

At one point, Shanann called her friend, Cristina Meacham, to talk about her husband's behavior. Shanann told Meacham that she felt unwanted because Chris constantly pushed her away. She wondered if his lack of affection was a sign that he was cheating on her.

Throughout the rest of the week, tensions flared between Chris and Shanann. At one point, Chris told his parents that he wanted to separate from Shanann. Meanwhile, Shanann continued to text Meacham and complain about Chris. She accused him of being too weak to stand up to his parents and defend her and the girls. She also said that Chris had not even asked about how she felt or how her pregnancy was going.

During one of their arguments, Chris told Shanann that he did not want the new baby. Upset, Shanann texted a few

Shanann had scheduled a gender reveal party for the new baby, but after another argument with Chris, she canceled it. Instead, she and Chris had a private gender reveal and found out that the new baby was a boy. Shanann texted a friend that they planned to name the baby Nico Lee Watts. She also said that Chris had agreed to try to work out the problems in their marriage.

friends and told them that she felt confused and scared. She
and Chris had never had problems like this before, and she did
not understand why he was acting so out of character.

Chris and Shanann's relationship continued to deteriorate
after the family returned to Colorado in early August. Chris
continued to be physically and emotionally distant from his
wife, which made her even more suspicious. She poured out
her feelings to friends, concerned that Chris might be having
an affair.

On August 9, Nickole Atkinson picked up Shanann and
drove to the Denver airport. The two women were traveling to
Scottsdale, Arizona, for a Thrive promoter training weekend.
While in Scottsdale,
Shanann texted Chris that
she loved and missed him.
During the trip, Shanann's
friends and coworkers
noticed that she was not
as upbeat and cheerful as
she usually was, and she seemed distraught over her marriage
problems. But Shanann seemed hopeful that when she
returned to Colorado, she and Chris would be able to sort out
their issues and emerge with their marriage stronger than ever.

When Shanann departed for Scottsdale, she left Chris a handwritten letter in which she expressed how much she wanted to fix their marriage.

CHAPTER SIX

CONCERNS MOUNT

S hortly after 2:00 p.m. on August 13, 2018, Chris arrived home in his work truck. Atkinson and Officer Coonrod were waiting for him in front of the house. Chris calmly walked over to Coonrod and introduced himself. Then Chris opened the garage door and entered the house alone. A few minutes later, he opened the front door to let Coonrod inside. While Coonrod started looking around the house, Chris calmed down the barking dog.

An Empty House

Coonrod glanced into the pantry and the living room but didn't find anyone. Next he turned on his flashlight and descended into the basement. Nobody was there either. Then Coonrod climbed the stairs to the bedrooms on the second floor.

Scottsdale, Arizona, was the last place Shanann had been before returning home from her business trip and going missing.

Chris appeared concerned. He told Coonrod that the girls'
blankets were missing. Nothing else seemed to be missing from
the house.

Meanwhile, Atkinson's son, Nicholas, found Shanann's
iPhone among the couch pillows. Chris appeared puzzled
that Shanann had left her phone behind and told the
officer that she used it constantly for her job. Chris entered
Shanann's passcode into the phone and checked for messages.
Meanwhile, Atkinson urged Chris to check his security cameras
to confirm what time Shanann had left for the playdate, as
Chris had told her earlier. Atkinson mentioned that Chris had
told another friend, Addy Molony, that Shanann had left in the
middle of the night. But Chris dismissed Atkinson's comments,
insisting that Shanann had still been at home when he
left for work that morning.

Chris told Coonrod that he usually left for work
between 5:30 a.m. and 6:00 a.m. Coonrod asked
Chris if he and Shanann were having any problems in their
marriage. Chris replied that they were separating and planned
to sell their house.

Coonrod, Chris, and Atkinson then walked into the master
bedroom. The curtains were closed, and all the bedding was

piled in the corner of the room. Immediately, Atkinson sensed that something was wrong. "Bad thoughts were going through my head," she later said. "[Chris] does all the laundry, so if he left for work, why was the bed stripped . . . if Shanann was still there sleeping in it?"[1]

The Neighbor's Video

Coonrod walked next door to Nathaniel Trinastich's house and asked to view his home security video. Coonrod, Trinastich, and Chris gathered in Trinastich's living room to watch the video on his television. The angle of Trinastich's camera captured footage of the driveway outside the Wattses' garage. At 5:17 a.m., the camera's motion detector sensed movement and began filming as Chris's Anadarko truck backed into the Wattses' driveway. Chris explained that he had backed his truck into the garage to load the tools, water jugs, and backpack that he would need for work that day. But Chris appeared nervous, shifting his weight back and forth as he spoke.

Next, Trinastich played the recording from 1:48 a.m., which showed Shanann walking into the house. These were the only two times the camera's motion detector had sensed movement outside the Wattses' house. There was no video footage of Shanann or the girls leaving the house that morning.

When the video ended, Chris stepped outside to talk to another police officer who had arrived at the house. Once Chris had left the room, Trinastich turned to Coonrod. "He's not acting right," he told the officer.[2] He said Chris was talking more than usual and acting suspiciously. Trinastich had never seen Chris moving gear in and out of the garage, as Chris claimed to be doing in the video. Trinastich also told Coonrod that he had overheard Chris and Shanann fighting. The last fight he overheard had occurred shortly before Shanann left for her trip.

More Questions

Detective Dave Baumhover from the Frederick Police Department arrived at the house at 2:35 p.m. He conferred with Coonrod and learned that Shanann's personal belongings, including her cell phone, purse, wallet, and wedding ring, were still in the house. The girls' medications were also still at the house. Baumhover and Coonrod went back into the Wattses' bedroom, where they examined the bedding for signs of a struggle. They found nothing.

Baumhover then asked Chris to tell him about the events of the morning, including when he had last seen Shanann and the girls. Chris told Baumhover that he had briefly woken up when Shanann arrived home from the airport at 1:48 a.m. Before he left for work, Chris had told Shanann that he wanted to separate. The conversation left them both upset and crying. Then he said Shanann told him she was taking the girls to a friend's house that day. He insisted that Shanann had never told him the name of the friend. When asked how Shanann and the girls had gotten to the playdate without her car, Chris said they must have gotten a ride with one of Shanann's friends.

Baumhover asked Chris where he had gone that morning. Chris explained that he had driven to an oil well site to check on a repair. Because no one was at the site when he arrived, there were no witnesses to confirm his arrival.

Next, Baumhover spoke with Atkinson. Atkinson was adamant that Shanann would never have voluntarily left the house without her phone, medications, or the girls' car seats. She also thought it was unusual that Chris had backed his truck into the garage that morning. He never did that, because the noise from the truck might wake up his daughters.

Dave Baumhover was the lead detective for the Watts case. Later, he told reporters that he was deeply affected by the case and had to take time off work to deal with the trauma it caused.

Coonrod requested a BOLO alert for Shanann, Bella, and Celeste. Officers spent several hours searching the neighborhood. They knocked on doors and asked neighbors if they had any information that might help locate the missing mother and her two girls.

No Sign of Struggle

Officer Matthew James arrived at the Wattses' home at 4:20 p.m. Chris signed a consent form that waived his right to require a search warrant. This authorized James, Coonrod, and Officer Jared Bakes to conduct a search of the Wattses' house and property. While the officers were inside the house, Chris waited on the porch with the family dog, Dieter.

The officers found the house to be clean and organized. They did not find anything that indicated there had been a physical struggle. As the officers left the house, they told Chris to call them if Shanann and the girls came home.

The News Spreads

Meanwhile, Shanann's friends and family grew more concerned as news of her disappearance spread. Several friends texted Chris to offer their support. Others posted messages on social media asking for prayers or information concerning the whereabouts of Shanann and her daughters. On Facebook, Frankie asked people to pray for his sister and nieces. Jeanna Dietz texted Chris, offering to come over and organize a search party for Shanann and the girls. But Chris declined, saying the police had told him he was not allowed to do that.

Several of Shanann's friends suspected Chris was somehow involved in her disappearance. They knew how stressed and upset Shanann had been feeling about her marriage. In a group text, some of Shanann's friends suggested that the police should look at Chris's computer and cell phone.

After the police left, Nick and Amanda Thayer arrived at the Wattses' home to support Chris. They were friends of

SEARCH WARRANTS

A search warrant is an order signed by a judge. It authorizes police officers to search for specific objects and materials at a designated location. To get a search warrant, officers must show a judge that they have probable cause to believe that the location contains evidence of criminal activity. If the judge agrees, they will issue a search warrant. In some cases, a search warrant is not required. If a property owner voluntarily consents to a search, as Chris did, the police do not need a search warrant.

the Watts family. As they talked in the kitchen, Chris paced back and forth. He told the Thayers that he had called local emergency rooms to see if he could find Shanann, Bella, and Celeste. Together, Chris and the Thayers brainstormed ideas about what to do next. When the Thayers suggested contacting the media to run a story, Chris turned down the idea. He said he did not want the media to portray him as the enemy.

After the Thayers left, Chris called Kessinger. He was calm on the phone, but he sounded concerned about his daughters. The pair talked and FaceTimed several times that night, spending hours on the phone.

Looking for Leads

Meanwhile, the police worked around the clock to find Shanann and the girls. Officer James called Shanann's friends to gather

Todd Norris was chief of the Frederick Police Department at the time of the Watts case. During the investigation, he spoke about the case at press conferences.

information that might help the police locate her. They told him about the troubled state of Shanann's marriage and her worries about Chris having an affair. Shanann's friends also described how upset Shanann had been on the trip to Arizona.

Police officers continued to search the neighborhood, talking to residents. But they did not find any leads that could help them locate Shanann, Bella, and Celeste. The Frederick police set up surveillance on the Wattses' home.

Detective Baumhover was convinced Chris knew more than he was telling them. "I knew something was really wrong when I went out there, and so did Officer Coonrod, which is why he called me," he said later. Baumhover needed to determine if Shanann had left the house with the kids or if something terrible had happened to them. "I had already made the decision that if she had not returned by the morning, we were going to initiate a full-blown investigation," he said.[3]

Criminology experts study criminals and crimes. Many say that in a missing person case, the first 72 hours are the most critical. After a person is reported missing, the likelihood of finding that person decreases with each passing hour. In the first 48 hours, investigators have the best chance of following up on leads and interviewing witnesses before their memories fade.[4] Investigators often try to generate awareness about the missing person early on in order to gather as many potential leads as possible. Even people who are unrelated to the missing person may have witnessed a small detail that is critical to finding the person.

SUSPICION

In the early morning of August 14, the Frederick police officially listed Shanann, Bella, and Celeste as missing persons. At 7:00 a.m., Detective Baumhover issued a press release asking the public for information about the missing mother and her daughters. Minutes later, reporters began calling Shanann's family and friends.

The Search Intensifies

By 9:00 a.m., the Frederick Police Department had set up a command room at police headquarters to gather information and coordinate a search. Baumhover was appointed the lead detective on the case. He called the Colorado Bureau of Investigation (CBI) and the Federal Bureau of Investigation (FBI) to help with the case.

The story of a missing pregnant woman and her two young daughters quickly attracted national attention. By midday, news

As news of the disappearance spread, many neighbors and well-wishers visited the Watts family home. Some spoke to reporters about their thoughts on the case.

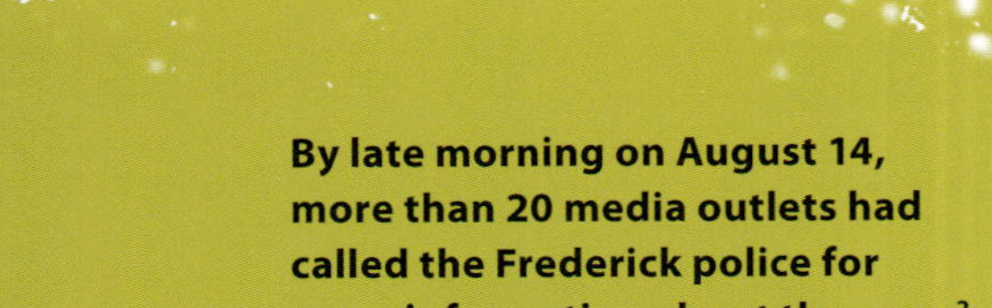

stories about the missing person case appeared online. During her lunch break at work, Kessinger found the breaking news stories online. She had spoken to Chris the day before, and he had told her that Shanann and the girls were missing. But he had seemed calm about it. After reading the news stories, Kessinger was shocked. She realized that Chris had lied to her. "When I read the news, I found out he was still married, and his wife was 15 weeks pregnant," Kessinger said. "I thought, 'If he was able to lie to me and hide something that big, what else was he lying about?'"[1]

Kessinger texted Chris and confronted him with the news stories. At first, he denied that Shanann's baby was his. But after Kessinger pushed him to tell the truth, Chris admitted that he was the baby's father. For the rest of the afternoon, Kessinger closely watched the online news coverage of the case.

COLORADO BUREAU OF INVESTIGATION

Formed in 1967, the CBI is a division of the Colorado Department of Public Safety. It assists local, county, and state law enforcement by providing forensic and laboratory services. CBI agents also assist in criminal investigations, including missing person cases, when requested by local and state law enforcement agencies.

Over many texts and calls, Kessinger urged Chris to tell her what he knew about his family's disappearance. Chris insisted he would never hurt his family. But to Kessinger, Chris appeared oddly unemotional about his missing wife and daughters. "It got to a point that he was telling me so many lies that I eventually told him that I did not want to speak to him again until his family was found," she said.[3] Then Kessinger deleted all of Chris's texts, photos, and videos from her cell phone.

The next day, Kessinger called the Weld County Sheriff's Office. She told them about her relationship with Chris and the lies he had told her. Later that day, Kessinger met with FBI detectives. "I just wanted to help," she said. "With a pregnant woman and two children missing, I was going to do anything that I could."[4]

K-9 Search

By midday on August 14, the Frederick police brought three search and rescue dogs to the Wattses' home. Inside the house, officers noticed vacuum lines on the carpet and the strong smell of cleaning chemicals. Chris allowed the K-9 dogs to search the house. While talking with Chris, the officers noted that he was acting strangely. He appeared emotionless, except when he smiled or smirked at inappropriate times.

Officers also took a cadaver dog inside the Wattses' home. Several times, the dog indicated that it had picked up the scent of human remains, but officers found nothing definitive. The cadaver dog also searched around Chris's work truck, which was parked outside the house. The dog indicated that it may have detected something near the truck. But because the truck was locked, the dog did not search inside it.

Agents Arrive

That afternoon, CBI and FBI agents arrived at the Frederick Police Department. After being briefed by Detective Baumhover, the agents began working on the case. CBI Agent Tammy Lee released an upgraded Missing/Endangered Alert for Shanann and the girls. She called Anadarko to get Chris's work cell phone data and truck GPS data. Lee also instructed Facebook and the wireless phone companies to preserve Shanann's and Chris's records and social media posts. The agents spent several days interviewing the Wattses' family members and friends, gathering information.

Meanwhile, Frederick police officers spread out over the Wyndham Hill neighborhood, where the

Watts family lived. They set up checkpoints and passed out missing person flyers to stopped drivers. Television news crews set up outside the Wattses' house and talked to anyone who knew the family.

Media Interviews

As police searched the Wattses' home and property with cadaver dogs, reporters gathered outside the house.

Police body cameras and reporters' cameras captured Chris's strange behavior at the Watts family home. Later, body language experts analyzed the footage.

Chris stood on the porch, answering their questions. In televised interviews, he pleaded for his family's safe return. "Shanann, Bella, Celeste, if you're out there, just come back, like if somebody has her, just please bring her back, I need to see everybody, I need to see everybody, again, this house is not complete without anybody here. Please bring them back," he pleaded.[5]

Chris also spoke about how difficult it was to be in the house while his family was missing. "This house isn't the same. Last night was traumatic. Last night—I can't really stay in this house again . . . with nobody here," Chris told reporters. "I wanted that knock on the door. I wanted to see those kids running, just barrel rush me and give me a hug and just knock me on the ground, but that didn't happen."[6]

Police Interview

Chris's television interviews ran on the 6:00 p.m. news on all four local TV networks. CBI agent Lee and FBI agent Grahm Coder watched the interviews with Detective Baumhover at the police station. They'd all had suspicions about Chris before the interviews, but now they were convinced that he knew more than he admitted. Detective Baumhover asked Coder to conduct a formal interview with Chris. They would have him come to the police station and take a polygraph test, also known as a lie detector test.

John Camper was director of the CBI at the time of the Watts case. He was involved in the investigation and spoke to the media at press conferences.

Shortly before 7:00 p.m., Baumhover called Chris and asked him to come to police headquarters. Chris agreed to come immediately. Then he called his parents in North Carolina and asked his father to come to Colorado. Chris left his home and headed to police headquarters, followed by police officers.

At police headquarters, Baumhover introduced Chris to Coder. Coder took Chris into an interview room and told him their conversation would be recorded. Lee sat in a nearby room, where she could watch a live video feed of the interview. To begin, Coder asked Chris to write down everything he remembered from when Shanann, Bella, and Celeste went missing. The FBI agent carefully went through Chris's statement for three hours, asking questions about everything.

While being questioned, Chris showed little emotion and did not ask about the status of the investigation. At one point, Coder noted that Shanann's friend Atkinson seemed more worried about Shanann and the girls than Chris did.

A few hours into the interview, Coder began to turn up the heat on Chris. He brought in photos of Shanann, Bella, and Celeste. He also asked Chris about an affair, which Chris denied. By showing Chris photos of his family and confronting him about his affair, Coder hoped to spark an emotional reaction from Chris.

Almost immediately, Coder noticed something striking as Chris looked at the photos. When Chris talked about his wife and daughters, he used the past tense. For example, he said that Celeste "was a girly girl." This was an immediate red flag for investigators. "If he is hoping and believing that they're still alive . . . why would you start talking about them in past tense?" said Lee.[8]

With their suspicions rising by the minute, investigators suggested that they stop the interview for the night. They asked Chris to return the next day for a polygraph test. They wanted him to be well rested before he took the test. They would also use the time before the polygraph test to search the Wattses' home again. Around 11:00 p.m., Chris walked out of the police station and went to Nick and Amanda Thayer's house, where he spent the night.

GETTING A CONFESSION

Ever since the police were first called to the Wattses' home, they had grown increasingly suspicious of Chris. The young husband was acting strangely, according to family and friends. His behavior, both on and off camera, did not match that of a husband and father consumed with worry about his missing family. Investigators hoped they could persuade Chris to reveal what had happened to his family.

Forensic Search

At 6:00 a.m. on August 15, police gathered at the Wattses' home to perform a forensic search. Officers photographed every room in the house. They sprayed luminol in the bedrooms, bathrooms, stairs, and garage entryway to detect blood. No blood was found. In the master bedroom, the pillowcases and

Neighbors and friends created a makeshift memorial outside the Watts family home. People brought stuffed animals, candles, and flowers in honor of Shanann and her daughters.

top sheet were found stuffed in a garbage can. However, the matching fitted sheet was missing. Officers also gathered the Watts family's computers, iPads, Apple Watches, and Amazon Echo and logged them as evidence.

At 8:00 a.m., the Anadarko security department called Agent Lee and reported that a review of Chris's work emails revealed he was having an affair with a coworker, Nikki Kessinger. The security department explained that Kessinger and Chris worked at the same office in Platteville, Colorado. According to the emails, their romantic relationship had begun in June 2018. The security department forwarded the emails to Lee, who ordered a complete examination of Kessinger.

Polygraph Test

The same morning, Chris's father, Ronnie, arrived in Colorado. He accompanied Chris to the Frederick police station at around 11:00 a.m. Ronnie waited in the hallway while Coder took Chris back to the interview room.

Lee was ready to administer a polygraph test in the interview room. Lee reassured Chris about the test and explained that polygraphs could sometimes make people nervous even if they were not hiding anything. Lee also explained that there were two ways to fail the test. Chris could fail the test if he did not follow the instructions. Or he could fail if he chose to tell a lie.

POLYGRAPH TESTS

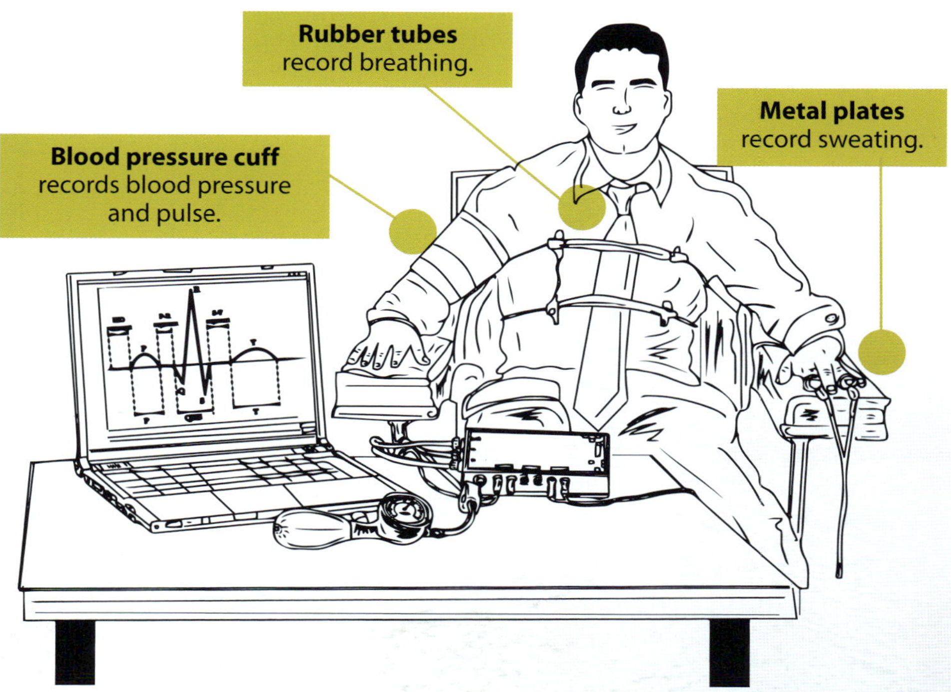

Polygraph machines are sometimes used by law enforcement to measure a person's physiological responses to questions. These machines include several different sensors that help them monitor a person's breathing, pulse, and blood pressure.

The well site Chris visited was called Cervi 319. Located north of Roggen, Colorado, the site is a cattle ranch with several oil and gas wells.

As Lee prepared Chris for the test, she asked him what he thought had happened to his family. Chris said that he initially believed Shanann was taking some time away from home at a friend's house. But now, he was uncertain and wondered if his family was in trouble. Lee prepped Chris with the questions she planned to ask him. He told her he thought he would have no problem passing the test.

At around 2:23 p.m., Lee hooked Chris up to the polygraph machine. She began with a directed-lie practice test, in which she instructed Chris to deliberately lie so that the polygraph machine could record his physical responses. Then Lee started the actual polygraph test. During the test, she asked Chris three questions. First, did he physically cause Shanann's disappearance? Second, was he lying about the last time he saw Shanann? And last, did he know where Shanann was now? Lee asked each question three times, measuring Chris's responses.[1] Then she left the room to grade the results.

The polygraph results suggested that Chris Watts was being deceptive. "The type of testing format that I used, we would consider someone to be deceptive if they were a -4 or below," Lee said. "Chris Watts scored -18."[2]

Well Site Search

While Chris was at the police station, CBI agents met with his Anadarko boss, Luke Epple. Epple took them to the remote well site that Chris had visited on the morning his family disappeared. Epple described the site's layout. It had an oil well head, a separator, and giant storage tanks on a gravel pad. Epple explained that the gas is pumped out to another location after the oil, gas, and water are separated. The oil and water mixture is stored in the giant holding tanks. Then the water is separated from the oil and funneled into the third, smaller tank.

The agents launched a drone and took aerial photographs of the site. The drone systematically searched the well site while the agents watched via video feed. In one area, they noticed what looked like a sheet on the ground. The officers walked over to the area for a closer look and found a fitted sheet that perfectly matched the bedding found at the Wattses' house. The sheet was stained with dirt as if it had been dragged on the ground. Two large black garbage bags lay nearby. There was also a rectangular area on the ground where it looked as if someone had recently been digging.

Caught in Lies

Around 4:00 p.m., Lee and Coder returned to the interview room. Coder placed a large photo of Bella and Celeste in front of Watts. Then Lee informed Chris that he had failed the polygraph test. At first, Chris insisted that he had not lied during the test and did not know what had happened to his family. But then he admitted that he had lied about cheating on Shanann. Chris told the agents about his relationship with Kessinger, and they told him they already knew about it.

To get Chris to open up more, Coder and Lee tried another tactic. They began to describe a scenario in which Shanann was the bad guy. "Vilifying Shanann, it's a technique that we can use to eventually get the actual truth," Lee explained. "We just needed to find Shanann and the girls."[3] Coder told Chris that he understood Shanann could be a controlling person who did not listen to her husband. The more the agents questioned Chris, the more confused and agitated he became. Then Chris asked to speak with his father. The agents hoped letting Chris have a conversation with his father would lead to a confession, so they allowed Ronnie to enter the interview room.

First Confession

Six hours after he arrived at the police station, Ronnie sat down with his son. They were alone in the interview room, but the agents watched their conversation via video feed. Chris told his father that he had failed the polygraph test, and then he told him about his affair. When pressed by Ronnie, Chris admitted to strangling Shanann.

But he said he had strangled Shanann in a rage after discovering that she had smothered their two daughters to get back at him for wanting to separate. "It was pretty much gut-wrenching to hear Chris talk about the fact that he murdered his wife to his own father," Lee said. "It was the theme of Shanann doing something to the girls, that I had just given him prior to leaving the room. But to actually hear that come out of his mouth, was shocking."[4]

After Chris disposed of his daughters' bodies, he called their school and unenrolled them.

As soon as Chris confessed to Shanann's murder, Coder and Lee entered the interview room. Although the agents doubted Chris's story about Shanann killing the girls, they tried to appear sympathetic to Chris. They still needed him to reveal the location of the bodies. After more questions, Chris finally admitted that he had buried Shanann in a shallow grave at one of Anadarko's well sites and put the girls' bodies in nearby oil and water tanks. He marked where he had put the bodies on a large drone photograph of the well site.

Recovering Shanann

After Chris confessed, the process of recovering the bodies of Shanann and her daughters began.

After obtaining a search warrant, crime scene analysts began documenting the crime scene. They took digital photographs and measurements of the area. They collected evidence, including the fitted sheet and two garbage bags.

Epple led CBI crime scene analysts up the stairs of the two oil holding tanks. They shone a flashlight into the tank through an eight-inch (20 cm) hatch.[5] But it was too dark to see anything. The analysts gathered several blond hairs found on the rim of one of the tank's hatches and entered them into evidence. They decided to drain both tanks the following day.

Later that evening, Detective Baumhover and Officer Coonrod arrived at the well site. Under lights, officers began to dig in the area where Watts had said Shanann's body was buried. Less than a foot under the surface, officers uncovered the body of an adult female, which they believed to be Shanann. The body was face down with her knees pulled to her chest. An amniotic sac that held the body of a fetus was also discovered. The Weld County coroner pronounced Shanann dead at 12:05 a.m. on August 16. Her body was sent to the medical examiner's office for an autopsy.

A little after 11:00 p.m., Chris was arrested and taken into police custody. He was brought to the Weld County Jail in Greeley, Colorado, where he was placed in a cell for the night. At 12:08 a.m., the Frederick Police Department announced

The process of recovering Bella's and Celeste's bodies from the oil tanks took almost 14 hours. Members of the recovery team had to work carefully while retrieving and lifting the fragile bodies out of the tanks.

that Chris had been arrested for the murders of his wife and daughters. His arrest quickly became headline news across the country.

Recovering the Girls

The same day, a team assembled at the well site for the gruesome task of recovering the girls' bodies from the two large tanks. Lee was part of the group. An Anadarko employee gave the team a safety briefing before the recovery efforts began.

The hazardous materials team from the Colorado State Patrol started draining the east tank first. Workers carefully drained the oil through metal screens to preserve any evidence. Once the tank was drained, the team removed the rear maintenance hole near the tank's base. A hazmat team member, Sergeant Luke Armstrong, climbed the stairs to the top of the tank and looked inside through a small hatch. He could see what looked like a body lying face down on the south side of the tank. Investigators took photos of the scene while troopers put on hazmat suits and breathing apparatuses. Removing the body was dangerous because the tank contained a significant amount of oil sludge and toxic fumes. People could stay in the tank for only a few minutes.

Trooper Darrin Reeder entered the tank first, followed by Trooper Otto Wilson. They located the body of a small female child, believed to be Celeste, and began the delicate process of removing her. Celeste's body was covered in oil. She was wearing a pink nightgown and a diaper.

Next, the team began draining the west tank, where they believed Bella's body was located. Once it was drained, two troopers entered the tank and found Bella's body. She was wearing a pair of pink pajamas and was covered in oil. They carefully removed her body from the tank. The bodies of both girls were driven to the morgue for autopsies.

Cause of Death

On August 17, forensic pathologist Dr. Michael Burson and his team began the autopsy of Shanann at the McKee Medical Center in Loveland, Colorado. That morning, Chris's defense attorney, James Merson, had filed an emergency motion requesting DNA swabs, X-rays, and fingernail scrapings from Bella and Celeste to recover any evidence that their mother had strangled them,

FORENSIC PATHOLOGISTS

A forensic pathologist is a medical doctor specially trained to perform autopsies on people who have died suddenly, unexpectedly, or violently. They are experts in determining the cause and manner of death. When performing autopsies, forensic pathologists look for evidence of disease, injury, or poisoning. They collect medical evidence such as secretions, hairs, and skin cells. Using this evidence, they can reconstruct how a person received injuries.

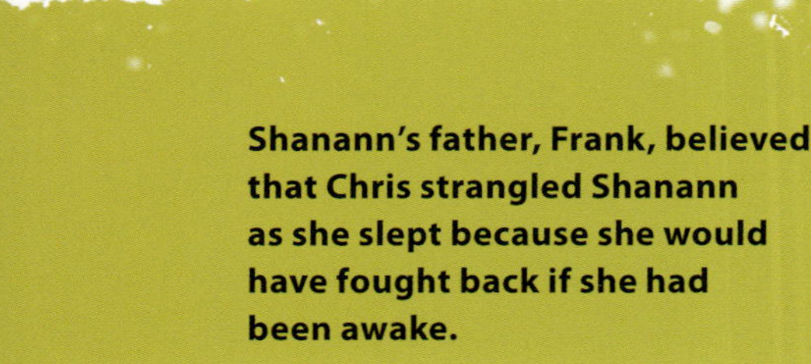

as Chris claimed. A judge denied the requests.

During Shanann's autopsy, Burson found bruising to the muscles and tissues in her neck. But the hyoid bone in her neck was not broken. Trauma to this U-shaped neck bone often occurs during strangulation. Burson found no other trauma to Shanann's body and no evidence of disease. He determined that Shanann had died from asphyxiation caused by manual strangulation. He ruled her death a homicide.

Next, Burson began the autopsy of Bella. The young girl had a lot of skin slippage, most likely from being in the oil tank for several days. Skin slippage is when the skin of a decomposing body separates and slips off. Burson also observed scrapes on Bella's buttocks and the tops of her shoulders. He noted that

THE FUNERALS

The Rzuceks arranged to bring the bodies of Shanann, Bella, and Celeste to North Carolina for funerals. Because the girls had been submerged in oil for days, they had to be put in sealed coffins so no dangerous gases could leak out from their bodies. On September 1, 2018, the family held a funeral mass for Shanann, Bella, and Celeste at a Catholic church in North Carolina. About 200 people attended the funeral. The service was also live streamed on Facebook.[7] After the funeral, Shanann, her daughters, and her unborn son were buried in a cemetery in Aberdeen, North Carolina.

On August 17, hundreds of mourners gathered outside the Watts family home for a candlelight vigil in honor of Shanann and the girls.

the skin that connected her top lip to her gums was torn, and her inner lip was bruised. She had also bitten into her tongue. These injuries led Burson to believe that Bella had struggled before she died. He determined that Bella's cause of death was asphyxiation due to smothering. Her death was also ruled a homicide.

Finally, Burson performed an autopsy on Celeste. Like her sister, she also had a significant amount of skin slippage. But unlike Bella, there was no sign of injury or bruising on Celeste's face, mouth, or neck. Burson ruled Celeste's death a homicide, most likely asphyxiation due to smothering.

CHAPTER NINE

LIFE WITHOUT PAROLE

On August 20, Weld County district attorney Michael Rourke announced that Christopher Watts was charged in the deaths of his wife and daughters. The next day, Chris appeared in court wearing an orange prison jumpsuit and shackles. He appeared emotionless as the charges against him were formally read. Chris was charged with five counts of first-degree murder in the deaths of Shanann, Bella, and Celeste. Prosecutors brought two murder charges against Chris for the deaths of each of his daughters because the girls were under 12 years old and Chris was in a position of trust. Chris was also charged with three counts of tampering with a deceased human body and one count of unlawful termination of a pregnancy.[1]

Frank and Frankie Rzucek sat in the front row of the courtroom. They watched Chris, who never looked at

When Chris appeared in court to hear the charges against him, he wore shackles on his wrists and ankles. He seemed calm and unbothered when the charges were read, only giving short responses such as "Yes, sir."

them directly. As the judge read the charges, Frank wept and covered his eyes with his hands while Frankie put his arm around him. If convicted on the first-degree murder charges, Chris faced a minimum sentence of life in prison and potentially the death penalty. Because of the seriousness of the charges against him, Chris would be held without bail until trial.

That afternoon, CBI agents interviewed Frank and Frankie at the Colorado hotel where they were staying. Agent Matthew Sailor asked the two men about Chris's relationship with Shanann and the girls. Frank told Sailor that Chris had always been a great father and husband, and he had never noticed any problems until Shanann and the girls visited North Carolina that summer.

But Frank insisted there was no way Shanann had hurt her daughters as Chris had claimed. "I don't believe that at all," he said. "She would never, ever hurt those kids." Frankie agreed that Chris had been a great brother-in-law, but he had also noticed a change in him that summer. And he could not understand why Chris had murdered his family. "It's like the devil got into him and turned him into a whole different person," Frankie said.[2]

A Guilty Plea

For weeks, the story of the Watts family murders made headlines around the country. Thousands of people scrolled through Shanann's Facebook posts. True crime fans posted theories about what had led Chris to murder his family. They searched social media and the internet for clues.

In early October 2018, Chris's defense team approached the district attorney's office about a potential plea deal. In a plea deal, the defendant agrees to plead guilty in exchange for a lighter sentence or reduced charges. District Attorney Rourke said he would consider a deal but refused to dismiss any of

As Frankie, *right*, comforted his weeping father during the court hearing, he was seen glaring at Chris. Frankie later said that Chris "stole his whole world" when he murdered Shanann and the girls.

the charges against Chris. Rourke and Deputy District Attorney
Steve Wrenn flew to North Carolina to discuss the potential of a
plea deal with Shanann's family.

The Rzuceks agreed to pursue a plea deal to remove the
possibility of the death penalty. Without a deal, the trial and
appeal process could drag on for years, especially in a death
penalty case. If a plea deal could be reached, it would give the
Rzucek family closure and allow them to move forward with
their lives.

On November 6, 2018, Chris, his defense team, and prosecutors appeared in a surprise court hearing to accept a plea deal. Chris would plead guilty to all charges against him in return for the prosecutors not seeking the death penalty. Chris entered the

courtroom in handcuffs and shackles, wearing a bulletproof
vest. Shanann's family sat on one side of the courtroom while
the Watts family sat on the other. As the judge read each
charge, Chris wept and pleaded guilty to each.

The Watts family was devastated that Chris accepted the
plea deal. They believed he had been coerced into accepting

the deal, and they were upset that Chris had not consulted
them about it first. In an interview before Chris's sentencing,
Cindy said she could not believe her son could kill his children.
Yet the possibility that it could be true terrified her. "That scares
me to death. It scares me to death to think that he could have
done all of this. And I don't wanna go there. I don't wanna go
there now," she said. Cindy also did not understand why Chris
accepted the plea deal. "I wouldn't," she said. "I'd fight. I'd fight
to the end. But then you ask yourself, would a normal person . . .
dispose of the bodies the way he did?"[3]

Life in Prison

On November 19, Chris Watts was officially sentenced to five
life sentences without the possibility of parole. He was also
sentenced to 48 years in prison for the unlawful termination
of a pregnancy and 36 years in prison for the disposal of the
bodies. "He deserves a
life sentence for each and
every act on top of one
another. It was important
that each of those
beautiful human beings be reflected in the ultimate sentence
that will be imposed," said District Attorney Rourke.[4]

Three women are killed by their current partner or ex-partner every day in the United States.[5]

Chris was transferred to the maximum-security Dodge
Correctional Institution in Waupun, Wisconsin. He is in

District Attorney Rourke was part of the prosecution team. In court, he spoke about Chris's motives and shared a detailed account of how Chris murdered his wife and daughters.

lockdown for 23 hours a day. For one hour each day, he is allowed to leave his cell for a shower or exercise.[6] He is allowed to keep a Bible and photos of his family in his cell. Chris reportedly spends most of his time reading the Bible and writing letters, mainly to women who wrote to him after his sentencing. He keeps pictures of Shanann, Bella, and Celeste on his cell wall and talks to them every night.

Sources said that Chris is treated as an outcast in the prison. "No one wants anything to do with him," a source told *People* magazine in 2021. "He's on the lowest social tier of the entire prison." The source added, "He's probably the most hated man in that prison, because he killed children. There's a definite pecking order in jail, and someone who hurts or kills kids is at the very bottom."[7]

A New Confession

For investigators, the question of why Chris murdered his family remains unanswered. "I don't expect that [Chris] will ever tell the truth about what truly happened or why," said District Attorney Rourke. "The best we can do is piece together some kind of understanding from the evidence that is available to us. The evidence tells us this: The defendant coldly and deliberately ended four lives, not in a fit of rage, not by way of accident, but in a calculated and sickening manner."[8]

To get answers, Agent Lee, Agent Coder, and Detective Baumhover went to Dodge Correctional Institution to talk to Chris in February 2019. They wanted him to reveal what had happened to his family. "I needed to hear him say that Shanann did not murder her children," Lee said. "I needed to have that come out of his mouth."[9]

During a five-hour interview, Chris finally told investigators the details of his family's last moments.[10] The truth was more

TRAUMA REMAINS

The Watts family murders have had a long-lasting impact on the investigators involved in the case. Some still experience nightmares about oil wells. Others cannot get the images of the wells where the Watts girls were found out of their minds. Detective Baumhover has dealt with post-traumatic stress disorder (PTSD) and flashbacks since his involvement in the case. Agent Lee entered counseling to help her deal with her experiences. And every time Weld County district attorney Rourke sees an oil well, he thinks of the Watts girls.

disturbing than they had imagined. Chris said he felt Shanann climb into bed after returning from her trip around 2:00 a.m., and he suspected that she knew about his affair. The couple had sex and then fell asleep.

As he got ready for work a few hours later, Chris woke Shanann up to talk. She began to cry and accused him of having an affair, which he denied. When Chris told her he wanted to end their marriage, Shanann threatened to take the girls away. At that point, Chris snapped and strangled her. "Every time I think about it, I'm just like, did I know I was going to do that before I got on top of her?" Chris said. "Everything that happened that morning I just don't—I don't know . . . like, I try to go back in my head. . . . I didn't want to do this, but I did it," he said.[11]

The noise from the fight woke up Bella, who asked Chris what was wrong with her mommy. Chris told his daughter that Shanann did not feel well. He wrapped Shanann's body in a sheet, dragged her downstairs, and loaded her into his truck. As he came back inside the house, Celeste woke up. Chris put both girls into the back seat of his truck and drove to the oil site.

Chris left the girls in the truck, pulled Shanann's body out, and buried her in a shallow grave. When he returned, he put Celeste's blanket over her head and strangled her. Bella was sitting beside her sister when this happened. Chris carried Celeste's body to one of the oil tanks and dropped her inside.

THE OIL WELL SITE

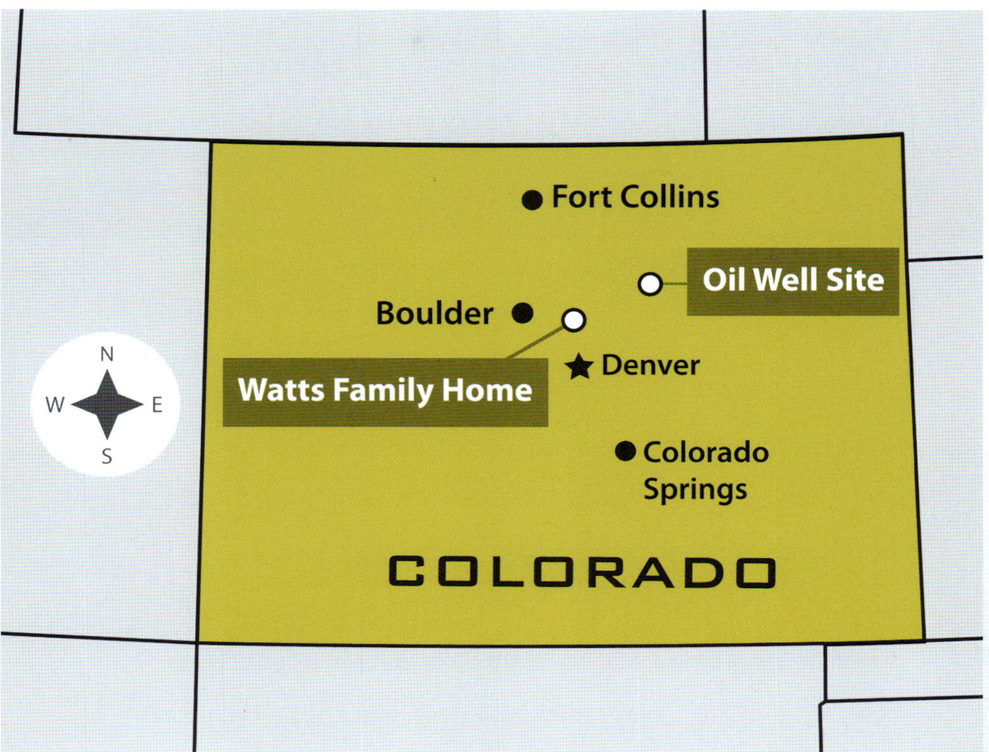

The oil well site where Chris disposed of his wife's and daughters' bodies was about 45 minutes away from the Watts family home.

Shanann, Bella, Celeste, and Shanann's unborn baby are buried at Bethesda Cemetery in North Carolina.

Then Chris returned to the truck. "What happened to CeCe?" Bella asked him. "Is the same thing gonna happen to me as CeCe?"[12] Chris put the blanket over Bella's head and smothered her as she fought back. Then Chris dropped Bella's body in the second oil tank. "Chris told us that, every night when he closes his eyes, he hears Bella yell, 'Daddy no!'" Lee said. "I feel like it's kind of what he deserves. I hope he hears that every night."[13]

Chris admitted that he decided to blame Shanann for the girls' murders during his questioning by police. When police mentioned the possibility that Shanann had harmed the girls, he decided to use it. However, Chris admitted the truth to his lawyers a few weeks later.

"Those are my kids, those are my babies," Chris said. "I talked to them every night. I don't see how this could happen.

Every time I see pictures of them now, I don't know how this could happen. Being a dad was the best part of my life. I took it all away."[14]

Aftermath

Chris Watts appeared to have a perfect life: a beautiful wife, two charming daughters, and a baby boy on the way. When his family went missing, he captured the country's attention as he pleaded for their return. Hours later, Chris would be arrested for murdering his entire family. As details emerged about the horrific crime, Chris's image as a family man was shattered.

Many people remain fascinated by the Watts family murders. Numerous books, articles, and documentaries have explored the case. In 2020, Netflix released *American Murder: The Family Next Door*. This documentary used social media posts, recordings, text messages, and home videos to examine the Watts case. The documentary's director, Jenny Popplewell, met with Shanann's family to get their approval on the project.

Many people praised the documentary for its skillful storytelling and its emphasis on Shanann. "It's not often that we so clearly get to see and hear the voice of the victim after the fact, but throughout *American Murder*, the power of Shanann's own voice is overwhelming," wrote Aja Romano, a film critic and culture writer. "It's loud, strong, and utterly blameless."[15]

TIMELINE

2010

- Shanann Rzucek and Christopher Watts meet via a mutual friend in North Carolina and begin dating.

2012

- Shanann and Chris move to Colorado and get married.

2013

- In December, Shanann and Chris welcome their first child, Bella Marie Watts.

2015

- Shanann and Chris file for bankruptcy.

- In July, the couple's second daughter, Celeste Cathryn "CeCe" Watts, is born.

2016

- Shanann signs up as an independent contractor for Le-Vel. She promotes Thrive, the company's lifestyle supplement. She turns to social media to document her life and promote her business.

2018

- In May, Shanann surprises Chris with the news that she is pregnant with their third child.

- In June, Chris talks to a coworker, Nikki Kessinger, for the first time. Their relationship quickly progresses into an affair.

- On June 26, Shanann, Bella, and Celeste travel to North Carolina for a six-week trip to visit family.

- On August 9, Shanann travels to Scottsdale, Arizona, for a business trip. She tells her friends that she suspects Chris is having an affair.

- On August 13, Shanann returns home from a business trip in the early morning hours. Later that morning, her friend Nickole Atkinson becomes concerned about not being able to reach Shanann. She calls police about the missing mother and her two daughters. Police talk to Chris and notice that he acts strangely.

- On August 14, Chris gives interviews that are broadcast on television. After watching the interviews, detectives are convinced that Chris is hiding information about his family's whereabouts. Agents conduct a formal interview of Chris at police headquarters.

- On August 15, Chris fails a polygraph test. He admits to killing Shanann but insists that he flew into a rage after she killed the girls. He tells investigators he buried Shanann in a shallow grave at one of Anadarko's well sites and put the girls' bodies in nearby oil tanks. Police arrest Chris for the murders of his wife and daughters.

- On August 16, police recover the bodies of Shanann and her unborn child. A hazardous materials team recovers the bodies of Bella and Celeste from oil tanks.

- On August 17, medical examiners perform autopsies on Shanann, Bella, and Celeste. All three deaths are ruled homicides.

- On August 20, Chris is formally charged with five counts of first-degree murder, three counts of tampering with a deceased human, and one count of unlawful termination of a pregnancy.

- On November 6, Chris pleads guilty to the murders of his wife and daughters.

- On November 19, Chris is sentenced to life in prison without the possibility of parole.

2019

- Investigators meet with Chris, and he admits to killing his daughters after he killed his wife.

2020

- Netflix releases *American Murder: The Family Next Door*, a documentary about the Watts family murders.

ESSENTIAL FACTS

SIGNIFICANT EVENTS

- On August 13, 2018, Shanann Watts, who is 15 weeks pregnant, disappears along with her daughters, four-year-old Bella and three-year-old Celeste.

- On August 14, Chris Watts pleads for his family's safe return in televised interviews. Investigators suspect that he knows something about his family's disappearance.

- On August 15, Chris fails a polygraph test. He eventually admits to killing his wife but insists he did so in a fit of rage after discovering that Shanann had killed the girls. Chris is arrested and charged with the murders of his wife and daughters.

- The remains of Shanann, Bella, and Celeste are found on August 16 on an oil well property of Chris's employer, Anadarko Petroleum.

- In November 2018, Chris pleads guilty to the murders and is sentenced to life in prison without parole.

- In February 2019, Chris gives a detailed account of his family's last moments and admits to killing his daughters after he killed his wife.

KEY PLAYERS

- Shanann Watts, a young wife and mother, went missing on August 13, 2018.

- Bella and Celeste Watts were the young daughters of Chris and Shanann Watts. They went missing on August 13, 2018.

- Christopher Watts was Shanann's husband and Bella and Celeste's father. He pleaded guilty to their murders and was sentenced to life in prison without the possibility of parole.

- Detective Dave Baumhover was one of the lead officers investigating the Watts case.

- Tammy Lee was an agent with the Colorado Bureau of Investigation. She questioned Chris and administered his polygraph test.

- Nikki Kessinger was Chris's coworker. Chris started an affair with her during the summer of 2018.

IMPACT ON SOCIETY

On the surface, Shanann and Chris Watts appeared to have the perfect marriage and family. But in 2018, the pregnant mother and her two daughters, Bella and Celeste, disappeared without a trace from their home. The story soon became national news. As search efforts yielded no significant leads, police became increasingly suspicious of Shanann's husband, Chris. The public was shocked when Chris confessed to murdering his family. It was revealed that Chris had been having an affair with a young coworker named Nikki Kessinger. Chris's cold and callous disposal of his wife's and daughters' bodies at an oil well site horrified investigators and members of the public.

Chris Watts was sentenced to life in prison without parole. Months later, he confessed that his daughters were still alive when he killed his wife and that Bella had fought for her life. During and after the investigation, the case captured the attention of both the public and the media, becoming a true crime obsession. This was in part due to how much Shanann had documented her family's life on social media, sharing numerous videos of her daughters and Facebook posts praising her husband. Many people were shocked to discover the tensions that had been lying underneath the surface of the family's picture-perfect social media image.

QUOTE

"I don't expect that [Chris] will ever tell the truth about what truly happened or why. . . . The best we can do is piece together some kind of understanding from the evidence that is available to us. The evidence tells us this: The defendant coldly and deliberately ended four lives, not in a fit of rage, not by way of accident, but in a calculated and sickening manner."

—*Michael Rourke, Weld County district attorney*

GLOSSARY

affair
A romantic or sexual relationship between two people when one or both parties are already in a committed relationship with someone else.

asphyxiation
Deprivation of oxygen that can result in death.

autopsy
An examination of a dead body to determine the cause of death.

bankruptcy
A legal process to help people who owe money get relief from debts they cannot pay.

cadaver
A dead human body.

commission
A sum of money paid to an employee upon completion of a task, such as selling a certain amount of goods.

coroner
An official who investigates suspicious, violent, or sudden deaths.

forensic
Characterized by the use of scientific techniques to investigate a crime.

hazmat
A shorthand term for hazardous materials.

homicide
The killing of one person by another.

independent contractor
A person who performs work for a business or organization under a contract but is not an employee.

luminol
A chemical that emits a blue glow when it comes in contact with blood.

polygraph test
A test that measures the body's physical response when being questioned. Police may interpret the results as proof of whether the person being questioned is lying.

ADDITIONAL RESOURCES

SELECTED BIBLIOGRAPHY

American Murder: The Family Next Door. Directed by Jenny Popplewell. Netflix, 2020.

Cadle, Cheryln. *Letters from Christopher: The Tragic Confessions of the Watts Family Murders*. Dorrance Publishing, 2019.

Glatt, John. *The Perfect Father: The True Story of Chris Watts, His All-American Family, and a Shocking Murder*. St. Martin's Press, 2020.

FURTHER READINGS

Harris, Duchess, JD, PhD, and Rebecca Rowell. *The History of Criminal Law*. Abdo, 2020.

Mooney, Carla. *The Murder of Laci Peterson*. Abdo, 2024.

Newquist, H. P. *Scene of the Crime: Tracking Down Criminals with Forensic Science*. Viking Books, 2021.

ONLINE RESOURCES

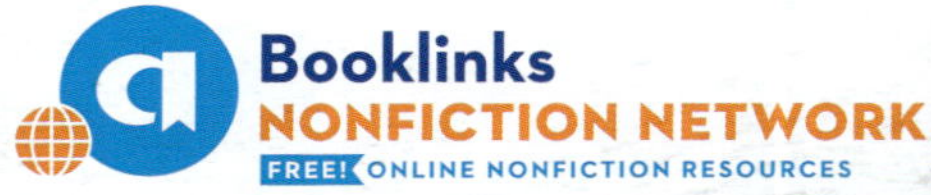

To learn more about the Watts family murders, please visit **abdobooklinks.com** or scan this QR code. These links are routinely monitored and updated to provide the most current information available.

MORE INFORMATION

For more information on this subject, contact or visit the following organizations:

AMERICAN ACADEMY OF FORENSIC SCIENCES (AAFS)

410 N. 21st St.

Colorado Springs, CO 80904

aafs.org

The AAFS is a professional society dedicated to promoting forensic science education and improving accuracy and precision in forensic science.

COLORADO BUREAU OF INVESTIGATION (CBI)

690 Kipling St., Ste. 3000

Lakewood, CO 80215

cbi.colorado.gov

Formed in 1967, the Colorado Bureau of Investigation (CBI) is a division of the Colorado Department of Public Safety. It assists local, county, and state law enforcement by providing forensic, laboratory, and investigative services across the state.

FEDERAL BUREAU OF INVESTIGATION (FBI)

935 Pennsylvania Ave. NW

Washington, DC 20535

fbi.gov

The Federal Bureau of Investigation (FBI) is the domestic intelligence and security service of the United States and its main federal law enforcement agency.

SOURCE NOTES

CHAPTER 1. MISSING

1. Kyle Peltz. "Video Shows Shanann Watts Shortly before Death." *CNN*, 20 Feb. 2019, cnn.com. Accessed 21 July 2023.

2. Steve Helling. "Shanann Watts Brother 'Always Worried about Her and the Girls' but 'Couldn't Protect Them.'" *People*, 1 Sept. 2018, people.com. Accessed 21 July 2023.

3. John Glatt. *The Perfect Father: The True Story of Chris Watts, His All-American Family, and a Shocking Murder*. St. Martin's Press, 2020. 3.

4. Karma Allen, Clayton Sandell, and Bill Hutchinson. "Friend of Colorado Woman Allegedly Killed by Husband Not 'Shocked' by His Arrest." *ABC News*, 20 Aug. 2018, abcnews.com. Accessed 21 July 2023.

5. Steve Helling. "The Day after Shanann Watts Was Killed, Friends Were Worried They Hadn't Heard from Her." *People*, 25 Jan. 2020, people.com. Accessed 25 July 2023.

6. Allen, Sandell, and Hutchinson, "Friend Not 'Shocked' by Arrest."

7. Glatt, *The Perfect Father*, 172.

8. Glatt, *The Perfect Father*, 175.

9. "How Prevalent Is Violence in Missing and Unidentified Persons Cases?" *National Institute of Justice*, 28 Feb. 2022, nij.ojp.gov. Accessed 25 July 2023.

CHAPTER 2. BUILDING A LIFE TOGETHER

1. John Glatt. *The Perfect Father: The True Story of Chris Watts, His All-American Family, and a Shocking Murder*. St. Martin's Press, 2020. 20–21.

2. Glatt, *The Perfect Father*, 19.

3. "About Lupus." *Lupus Research Alliance*, n.d., lupusresearch.org. Accessed 15 Aug. 2023.

4. Jeff Truesdell. "Shanann Watts Met Husband Chris Online during Dark Period 8 Years before Murder." *People*, 21 Aug. 2018, people.com. Accessed 25 July 2023.

5. Glatt, *The Perfect Father*, 8–10.

6. Sady Swanson. "Christopher Watts and Shanann Watts: Their Friends Saw a 'Perfect' Family. What Happened?" *Coloradoan*, 16 Nov. 2018, coloradoan.com. Accessed 25 July 2023.

7. Glatt, *The Perfect Father*, 29.

8. Glatt, *The Perfect Father*, 30.

9. Steve Helling. "Summer before Triple Murder, Watts Couple Had 'Full-Blown Fight' – Then Hugged When They Were Seen." *People*, 31 Aug. 2018, people.com. Accessed 25 July 2023.

CHAPTER 3. THE PERFECT FAMILY

1. John Glatt. *The Perfect Father: The True Story of Chris Watts, His All-American Family, and a Shocking Murder.* St. Martin's Press, 2020. 39–40.

2. Glatt, *The Perfect Father*, 41.

3. Kaitlyn Schallhorn. "Colorado Couple Had Deep Financial Troubles Years before Alleged Murders." *Fox News*, 17 Aug. 2018, foxnews.com. Accessed 25 July 2023.

4. Glatt, *The Perfect Father*, 45–46.

5. Schallhorn, "Couple Had Deep Financial Troubles."

6. Glatt, *The Perfect Father*, 52–53.

7. Glatt, *The Perfect Father*, 66.

CHAPTER 4. TROUBLE UNDER THE SURFACE

1. John Glatt. *The Perfect Father: The True Story of Chris Watts, His All-American Family, and a Shocking Murder.* St. Martin's Press, 2020. 60.

2. Glatt, *The Perfect Father*, 82.

3. Glatt, *The Perfect Father*, 90.

4. Glatt, *The Perfect Father*, 90.

5. Madeline St. Amour. "Christopher and Shanann Watts' Neighbors Heard Them 'Flat-Out Screaming.'" *Times-Call*, 30 Nov. 2018, timescall.com. Accessed 25 July 2023.

6. Steve Helling. "Summer before Triple Murder, Watts Couple Had 'Full-Blown Fight' – Then Hugged When They Were Seen." *People*, 31 Aug. 2018, people.com. Accessed 25 July 2023.

7. Ashley Collman. "From a Happy Pregnancy Announcement to a Shallow Grave: The Full Timeline of the Chris Watts Murder Case." *Insider*, 11 Oct. 2020, insider.com. Accessed 25 July 2023.

8. Glatt, *The Perfect Father*, 99.

9. Rory Tingle and Jennifer Smith. "Chilling Video Shows Christopher Watts' Daughter Singing about Her Dad before She Was Murdered." *New Zealand Herald*, 17 Aug. 2018, nzherald.co.nz. Accessed 25 July 2023.

SOURCE NOTES CONTINUED

CHAPTER 5. THE OTHER WOMAN

1. Elise Schmelzer. "'It's Horrific': Christopher Watts' Girlfriend Speaks Out for the First Time as Sentencing in Frederick Murders Draws Near." *Denver Post*, 15 Nov. 2018, denverpost.com. Accessed 25 July 2023.

2. John Glatt. *The Perfect Father: The True Story of Chris Watts, His All-American Family, and a Shocking Murder.* St. Martin's Press, 2020. 107.

3. Glatt, *The Perfect Father*, 108.

4. Shireen Khalil. "Killer Dad Chris Watts: 'If I Hadn't Met Nikki, I Would Never Have Killed My Family.'" *New Zealand Herald*, 3 Oct. 2019, nzherald.co.nz. Accessed 25 July 2023.

5. Glatt, *The Perfect Father*, 111.

6. Natalie Finn. "The Unraveling of Chris Watts before He Murdered His Family." *E! News*, 13 Aug. 2021, eonline.com. Accessed 25 July 2023.

CHAPTER 6. CONCERNS MOUNT

1. John Glatt. *The Perfect Father: The True Story of Chris Watts, His All-American Family, and a Shocking Murder.* St. Martin's Press, 2020. 177.

2. Jill Sederstrom. "The Neighbor Who Suspected Chris Watts from the Beginning." *Oxygen*, 16 July 2019, oxygen.com. Accessed 25 July 2023.

3. Glatt, *The Perfect Father*, 191.

4. Julia Jacobo. "Why the First 72 Hours in a Missing Persons Investigation Are the Most Critical, According to Criminology Experts." *ABC News*, 8 Oct. 2018, abcnews.com. Accessed 25 July 2023.

CHAPTER 7. SUSPICION

1. Elise Schmelzer. "'It's Horrific': Christopher Watts' Girlfriend Speaks Out for the First Time as Sentencing in Frederick Murders Draws Near." *Denver Post*, 15 Nov. 2018, denverpost.com. Accessed 25 July 2023.

2. John Glatt. *The Perfect Father: The True Story of Chris Watts, His All-American Family, and a Shocking Murder.* St. Martin's Press, 2020. 195.

3. Schmelzer, "Christopher Watts' Girlfriend Speaks Out."

4. Schmelzer, "Christopher Watts' Girlfriend Speaks Out."

5. Blair Miller. "Video: Chris Watts Pleads for Kids, Wife to Return Day before His Arrest in Their Murders." *Denver7*, 16 Aug. 2018, denver7.com. Accessed 25 July 2023.

6. "Former FBI Profiler: Suspect's Televised Plea for Slain Family's Return Shows 'Arrogance.'" *CBS News*, 17 Aug. 2018, cbsnews.com. Accessed 25 July 2023.

7. "Suspect's Plea for Slain Family's Return."

8. Alyssa Ray. "Here's How Investigators Got Chris Watts to Confess to Murdering His Family." *E! News*, 7 Dec. 2019, eonline.com. Accessed 25 July 2023.

CHAPTER 8. GETTING A CONFESSION

1. John Glatt. *The Perfect Father: The True Story of Chris Watts, His All-American Family, and a Shocking Murder.* St. Martin's Press, 2020. 223–225.

2. Chanel Vargas. "The Truth behind Chris Watts's Polygraph Score in Netflix's American Murder Documentary." *Yahoo*, 28 Sept. 2020, yahoo.com. Accessed 25 July 2023.

3. Alyssa Ray. "Here's How Investigators Got Chris Watts to Confess to Murdering His Family." *E! News*, 7 Dec. 2019, eonline.com. Accessed 25 July 2023.

4. Ray, "How Investigators Got Chris Watts to Confess."

5. Rebecca Powell, Jennifer Hefty, and Sady Swanson. "Chris Watts Murder Case: Potential Motive, Evidence Revealed in Court." *Coloradoan*, 19 Nov. 2018, coloradoan.com. Accessed 25 July 2023.

6. Jeff Truesdell. "See Photos of 'Monster' Chris Watts and Mistress – Who Searched For Wedding Dresses Days before Murders." *People*, 28 Nov. 2018, people.com. Accessed 25 July 2023.

7. Bryan Mims and Alfred Charles. "Shanann Watts Funeral: Family, Friends Gather in Moore County to Pay Final Respects." *WRAL News*, 1 Sept. 2018, wral.com. Accessed 25 July 2023.

CHAPTER 9. LIFE WITHOUT PAROLE

1. Alex Johnson and Erik Ortiz. "Christopher Watts, Charged with 5 Counts of Murder, Accused Wife of Killing Their Daughters, Police Say." *NBC News*, 20 Aug. 2018, nbcnews.com. Accessed 25 July 2023.

2. John Glatt. *The Perfect Father: The True Story of Chris Watts, His All-American Family, and a Shocking Murder.* St. Martin's Press, 2020. 266–267.

3. Kevin Vaughan. "Chris Watts' Parents Question Plea Deal in Murder of Wife, Daughters." *9News*, 19 Nov. 2018, 9news.com. Accessed 25 July 2023.

4. Christina Morales. "What to Know about Chris Watts and 'American Murder.'" *New York Times*, 16 Oct. 2020, nytimes.com. Accessed 25 July 2023.

5. "The Silent Epidemic of Femicide in the United States." *Sanctuary for Families*, 10 Mar. 2023, sanctuaryforfamilies.org. Accessed 25 July 2023.

6. Jessica Sager. "Where's Chris Watts Now? How Shanann Watts' Killer Spends His Time in Prison." *Parade*, 22 May 2023, parade.com. Accessed 25 July 2023.

7. Steve Helling. "Chris Watts Spends 36th Birthday in Prison: 'He's an Outcast, Even among Criminals,' Says Source." *People*, 16 May 2021, people.com. Accessed 25 July 2023.

8. Chelsea Robinson. "Prosecutors: Autopsy Shows 4-Year-Old 'Fought for Her Life' as Father Strangled Her." *KCRA 3*, 20 Nov. 2018, kcra.com. Accessed 25 July 2023.

9. Alyssa Ray. "Here's How Investigators Got Chris Watts to Confess to Murdering His Family." *E! News*, 7 Dec. 2019, eonline.com. Accessed 25 July 2023.

10. Sady Swanson. "Chris Watts Confesses to Killing Daughters for First Time: 'I Didn't Want to Do This, but I Did It.'" *Coloradoan*, 1 Oct. 2020, coloradoan.com. Accessed 25 July 2023.

11. Swanson, "Chris Watts Confesses to Killing Daughters."

12. Swanson, "Chris Watts Confesses to Killing Daughters."

13. Ray, "How Investigators Got Chris Watts to Confess."

14. Swanson, "Chris Watts Confesses to Killing Daughters."

15. Aja Romano. "Netflix's American Murder Is Mesmerizing Even if You're Already Familiar with the Watts Murders." *Vox*, 1 Oct. 2020, vox.com. Accessed 25 July 2023.

INDEX

ABOUT THE AUTHOR

CARLA MOONEY

Carla Mooney is a graduate of the University of Pennsylvania. Today, she writes for young people and is the author of many books for young adults and children. Mooney enjoys reading about true crime and forensic investigations.